More Summer Weekends Cookbook

COTTAGE LIFE'S

MORE SUMMER WEEKENDS
Cookbook

A WHOLE NEW COLLECTION OF RELAXING RECIPES,
GREAT TIPS, AND ENTERTAINING IDEAS

BY JANE RODMELL

Cottage Life BOOKS

© Copyright 2001 by Cottage Life Books

Library of Congress Cataloguing in Publication Data is available.

Canadian Cataloguing in Publication Data

Rodmell, Jane, 1938 –
    Cottage life's more summer weekends cookbook: a whole new collection of relaxing recipes, great tips, and entertaining ideas

Includes index.

ISBN 0-9696922-3-4

1. Cookery. I. Title. II. Title: More summer weekends cookbook.

TX829.R62 2001   641.5'64   C00-932996-X

Edited by Ann Vanderhoof
Design by Steve Manley, Overleaf Design Ltd.

Photography by Robert Wigington

Film by Colour Technologies,
Toronto, Ontario

Printed and bound in Canada by
D.W. Friesen & Sons Ltd., Altona, Manitoba

Published by
Cottage Life Books
54 St. Patrick St.
Toronto, Ontario, Canada
M5T 1V1
Published in the United States by
Cottage Life Books
Box 1338
Ellicott Station
Buffalo, N.Y., U.S.A. 14205
www.cottagelife.com

Trade distribution by
Firefly Books Ltd.
3680 Victoria Park Avenue
Willowdale, Ontario, Canada
M2H 3K1
and
Firefly Books (U.S.)
Box 1338
Ellicott Station
Buffalo, N.Y., U.S.A. 14205
www.fireflybooks.com

To Alex and Kate, with love

All recipes by Jane Rodmell, except as noted below:

Herbed Focaccia, p. 123: David Moore
Can't-Resist Chelsea Buns, p. 143: David Moore
The Ultimate Bran Muffin, p. 148: Jill Snider
Chocolate Banana Cake, p. 156: Jill Snider

Ice Cream Desserts, p. 163, 166, 167, 170, 171, 182, 183: Jill Snider
Lynda's No-Bake Bars, p. 157: Lynda van Velzen

The following recipes (or variations) were winners in *Cottage Life* magazine's annual recipe contest:

Asian Chicken with Oriental Noodle Salad, pp. 84–86: Susan Watson Cleveland
Barbecued Pork Tenderloin with 3-3-3 Sauce, p. 56: Gaylen Racine
Blueberry Brunch Cake, p. 168: Rita Lammers
Cedar-Smoked Salmon & Trout, p. 60: Gaylen Racine

Cottage Canoes, p. 31: Fran Stephen
Easy Cantaloupe Soup, p. 129: Susan Steinberg
Green Beans & Feta, p. 77: Nancy Weese
Grilled Eggplant Rounds, p. 27: Sue Enns
Grilled Pound Cake with Warmed Strawberries, p. 176: Nancy Weese
Overnight French Toast, p. 150: Danielle Stewart
Very, Very Green Salad, p. 88: Karen Dolan

Illustrations by Heather Holbrook

All photography (including cover) by Robert Wigington, except:
Author photograph, back cover, by Paul Orenstein; Fresh Vegetable Stew, p. 109, by Kevin Hewitt

Food styling by Ruth Gangbar and Jill Snider. Propping by Maggi Jones

Additional food styling by Claire Stancer and Sue Henderson; additional propping by Catherine MacFadyen, Sue Florian, and Lara McGraw Curry. Design assistant: Emese Ungar

*Front cover photo (clockwise from front): Grilled Garlic Shrimp for Lazy Summer Paella (p. 41),
Summer Vegetable Kebabs (p. 51), Peppered Sirloin (p. 57), Grilled Asparagus (p. 50), Roasted Garlic (p. 50),
Versatile Pound Cake with Berries (p. 175), Tuscan Pepper & Tomato Salad (p. 74), Dilly Potato Skewers (p. 58).*

Introduction

This book is designed to help you prepare meals that are delicious and uncomplicated. It contains a whole summer's worth of ideas for entertaining friends and relatives, and feeding the family, too – relaxed, contemporary recipes for great-tasting *easy* food based on fresh seasonal ingredients. After all, the cook wants to enjoy those precious summer days along with everyone else!

This new collection continues the features readers told me they loved – and used – in my last book, *Cottage Life's Summer Weekend Cookbook*, as well as including some new and expanded ones. Many of the dishes can be made partly or even entirely ahead – the tips with the recipes tell you how – so you're not left with a lot of last-minute fuss in the kitchen. The recipes are flexible, and include ideas for variations and substitutions for those times you don't have a particular ingredient on hand. There are suggestions for what to serve with various dishes – making it easy to put together a whole meal. (Look for the menu suggestions at the start of each recipe and in the contents pages that open each of the book's seven sections.) And there are plenty of other tips along the way to help you turn out fabulous food.

You'll find lots of new ideas for meatless meals, as well as suggestions for multi-generation gatherings. This collection also reflects the huge variety of grains and legumes now available in stores. And while the flavours of the Mediterranean remain a favourite, you'll notice Thai, Malaysian, and Indonesian influences in these pages as well – simplified recipes that use the flavours of these increasingly popular cuisines.

Many of the recipes in *More Summer Weekends Cookbook* were developed first for my column in *Cottage Life* magazine. Consequently, they don't rely

Jane Rodmell's "Cottage Cook" column appears regularly in *Cottage Life* magazine. Published six times a year, *Cottage Life* is full of practical information and entertaining reading about cottage (a.k.a. cabin, camp, chalet, vacation home) living. For subscription information, contact:

Cottage Life, 54 St. Patrick St., Toronto, Ontario, Canada M5T 1V1; tel.: 416-599-2000; fax: 416-599-0800; www.cottagelife.com

on a lot of fancy kitchen equipment. Although a food processor or blender often makes life easier (especially when cooking for large groups), I still rely on my good chopping knife and trusty pestle and mortar. These recipes also don't depend on a limitless supply of gourmet goodies, but rather use a core group of basic ingredients supplemented by fresh seasonal vegetables and fruit, meat, and fish.

The preparation and enjoyment of good food is best shared with good friends – likewise, the creation of a cookbook. My sincere thanks go to Ann Vanderhoof and Steve Manley, a creative editorial/design team without equal; to Penny Caldwell, Dave Zimmer, and the folks at *Cottage Life* magazine for their encouragement of editorial excellence, patience, and good humour; to incomparable food photographer Bob Wigington; and to my inspiring and much-appreciated cooking companions – among them, Jill Snider, Lynda van Velzen, David Moore, and the talented chefs and bakers at All the Best.

A few ingredients to help make meals sing

Beyond the basics, here are some special ingredients that are useful to have on hand. You'll be surprised what a difference in taste they can make:

Kosher or sea salt: This coarse-grained, additive-free salt is available in specialty stores and well-stocked supermarkets. It's about 20% less "salty" than iodized table salt and has a purer taste. With its coarser grains, it's ideal for barbecue rubs and sprinkling on foods during grilling.

Olives: Not the canned, pitted black ones. They can't compare in taste or texture with the intensely flavoured olives sold in bulk in some delis and supermarkets as well as in specialty stores: fruity black kalamatas, sharp cracked green ones, wrinkled sun-dried ones from Morocco, small ripe ones from Italy, ones with herbs or hot chilies. Good olives make a lively snack, add flavour to salads, and can be turned into tapenade, a tasty spread.

Parmesan cheese: Buy a chunk of the real Parmesan, Reggiano, and taste the difference. It has a rich nutty flavour the others don't approach. Serve it sprinkled on soup, grated over pasta, slivered on a salad or antipasto plattter, or just to nibble as a special snack.

TABLE OF CONTENTS

At the start of each section, you'll find a complete list of the recipes included in that section, as well as menus, tips, and serving suggestions.

THE ASIAN CUPBOARD:

This book includes some recipes with Asian flavours – Thai, Indonesian, Malaysian, Indian. Having a few basic staples on hand will make preparing them easy. Most of the following are now readily available in the oriental section of large supermarkets, and all except the fresh stuff have a long shelf or refrigerator life:

• Soy sauce

• Rice vinegar

• Pure sesame oil

• Dried rice-paper wrappers (great for making various seafood and vegetable rolls)

• Canned baby corn and water chestnuts, for adding instant oriental crunch to salads and stir fries

• Sambal oelek – a particular favourite in my family – or another hot red chili paste

• Spice pastes, a great shortcut for making curries as well as marinating food for the grill (you can also mix them with sour cream or yogurt for a quick dip); let the ingredient list on the jar be your guide: good-quality pastes include few additives and lots of real herbs and spices

• Fresh ginger, garlic, coriander, and lemon grass (look for lemon grass in your supermarket's fresh-herb section, or you can substitute a combination of lemon juice and zest)

Fresh herbs: They *really* make a difference. Fresh parsley – preferably the Italian flat-leaf variety – coriander (also known as cilantro), basil, mint, and dill are the five most frequently called for here (the dried variety of these herbs is usually not a satisfactory substitute), with oregano, rosemary, thyme, and tarragon making occasional appearances. To give fresh herbs the longest possible life, wash, spin dry in a salad spinner, wrap loosely in paper towel, and store in a roomy plastic bag in the vegetable crisper of your refrigerator. (If the leaves get bruised, they spoil quickly.) Better still, plant a few pots of herbs, so you can pick them as you need them.

Sun-dried tomatoes, dried porcini mushrooms, and dried cranberries, cherries, and blueberries: They keep almost forever on the shelf and add intense flavour. Yes, they're expensive – but a little goes a long way.

An assortment of fine condiments: Although you can use a good red or white wine vinegar for all the recipes in this book, give yourself some variety by adding a few others to your shelf, such as sweet, mild rice vinegar and balsamic. Supplement a basic vegetable oil with a light, fruity olive oil and sesame oil at the very least. Although there's a website offering more than 300 different mustards, a good Dijon (Maille or Grey Poupon) and a box of Keen's powdered mustard should serve nicely. On the sweet side, don't forget the real maple syrup.

A good selection of grains and legumes: Wheat berries, couscous, corn-meal; chickpeas, lentils, white beans; and rice in varieties beyond simple long-grain – basmati, arborio, brown, and wild.

(For tips on what to keep in the cupboard for making the desserts in this book, see "Stocking the Sweet Pantry," p. 155.)

And one final word on ingredients: Although these recipes rely heavily on healthy fresh produce, legumes, and grains, you'll note that cream crops up occasionally. So too do sour cream and butter. In most cases, the amount called for is modest, and the result is an enormous taste dividend. However, you can always substitute a lower-fat product if you like. And, yes, there are some rich, special-occasion dishes and desserts contained within. After all, what's a summer weekend without an occasional splurge?

BARBECUING WITH INDIRECT HEAT:

• Great for larger cuts of meat or bone-in chicken. With this method, the meat is cooked without a direct flame under it, so your dinner doesn't turn out charred on the outside and raw inside.

With a gas barbecue, preheat the barbecue to high with all burners on and the lid down. Place a foil drip pan on the rocks over one burner. When the barbecue is preheated, turn off the burner under the drip pan, put the meat on the grill above the pan (and the unlit burner) and close the lid. The heat from the lit burner(s) then circulates throughout the barbecue, cooking the meat. (The technique may vary slightly with some makes of barbecue, so check the manufacturer's instructions.)

With a covered charcoal grill, place a foil pan in the bottom and bank the coals on either side of it. Put the meat on the rack over the pan, and set the cover in place. Add more fuel to each side every hour or so of cooking time. Preferably, preheat these coals in a small Hibachi or metal chimney so they are ready when needed and the heat remains constant.

Get the heat out of the kitchen

Cooking outdoors is an essential part of summer, and a good number of the recipes in this book (including all of Section II) use the barbecue or provide an option for barbecue cooking. For the true grillmeister, barbecuing is an art form; for the more casual practitioner, here are some refresher tips:

• Remove food from the refrigerator a half-hour before grilling, so it will cook more quickly and evenly.

• When cooking marinated meats, pat them dry before putting them on the grill. This will help them brown.

• Always preheat the barbecue. Brush the grill rack vigorously to make sure it is clean, and oil lightly just before putting on the food.

• Place an oven thermometer inside your barbecue if it doesn't have an accurate one on the lid. Have an instant-read thermometer, too – it's the best way to tell when a large cut of meat is done the way you like it.

• Get yourself a good pair of stainless-steel hinged tongs (available in restaurant-supply stores). A vegetable grilling basket is also a handy barbecue accessory, as you can use it for grilling all sorts of small delicate food (including mussels, clams, and small fish).

• If you baste with the marinade in which raw meat, chicken, or fish has been sitting, make sure the meat continues to cook on the grill for at least a couple of minutes after basting. Don't serve the marinade as a sauce or glaze the meat with it after cooking unless you first bring it to a boil and simmer it for 5–10 minutes.

• For smoke flavour, soak chips of hardwood such as hickory, mesquite, apple, or cherry in water for an hour before using. Or use branches of aromatic herbs such as thyme, rosemary, or sage. Drain and place directly on the coals of a charcoal fire; with a gas grill, place wood in a shallow metal container (such as an aluminum pie plate) with holes punched in it and put the container on the rocks over the flame.

I. APPETIZERS, STARTERS, & SUNDOWN SNACKS

CONTENTS

Toasted Rosemary Walnuts (p. 21)

QUICK TRICKS

IN OTHER CHAPTERS...

More to Whet the Appetite

These recipes, which you'll find in other sections of the book, also work well as hors d'oeuvres or party snacks:

** These recipes use the barbecue, or have
an option for barbecue cooking*

Planning Sessions

As a rough guide when planning a happy-hour spread, have 5 choices: 3 cold or at room temperature, which can be ready for the table instantly, and 1 or 2 hot bites – one to be heated in the oven and the other to create action around the grill. The grilled finger food will be the most popular, so plan 3–5 pieces per person.

Cottage Canoes (p. 31)

CROWD PLEASERS

"Come for Drinks"

Invite friends to join you on the deck at sunset. This happy-hour spread is substantial enough to double as dinner, and everything can be prepared ahead – just grill the satays and skewers at the last minute.

Tamari Almonds *(p. 21)*

Easy Thai-Style Shrimp Rolls *(p. 22)* **with warm Peanut Dipping Sauce** *(p. 24)*

Steamed or blanched asparagus with Light Dipping Sauce *(Variation, p. 24)*

South Seas Chicken Satays *(p. 52)* **with warm Peanut Dipping Sauce** *(p. 24)*

Spicy Lemon Garlic Shrimp and Scallop Skewers *(p. 63)*

"Bring the Kids"

Casual happy-hour fare that will leave adults and kids (and the cook) happy. Pop the pizzas in the oven, then put the wings on the grill. Everyone is sure to be drawn to the barbecue by their delicious aroma.

Maple-Glazed Wings *(p. 66)*

Mini-Pizzas with Adult and Kid-Friendly Toppings *(pp. 124, 130, 131)*

Grilled Polenta Circles *(p. 28)* **with Roasted Tomato Corn Salsa** *(p. 20)*

Corn chips with Roasted Tomato Corn Salsa *(p. 20)*

Thin sticks of fresh vegetables with Three-Pepper Chip Dip *(p. 31; adjust heat to suit the crowd)*

A Middle Eastern Happy Hour

Red Pepper & Feta Spread *(p. 32)* **and Hummus** *(p. 13)* **with wedges of warm pita bread**

Assorted olives

Grilled Eggplant Rounds with Artichoke & Feta Topping *(p. 27)*

Mini Grilled Lamb Koftas *(p. 55)* **with Taratoor Sauce** *(p. 67)* **or Mint Yogurt Sauce** *(p. 67)*

A Mediterranean Get-Together

Roasted Pepper Pesto *(p. 14)* **with deli-style cream cheese or creamy goat cheese**

Cottage Tapenade *(p. 16)*

Grilled sliced Herbed Focaccia *(p. 123)* **or grilled baguette slices**

Bocconcini Bites *(p. 27)*

Pieces of grilled hot or mild Italian sausage or mini Wine-Marinated Lamb or Steak Kebabs *(p. 38)*

Caramelized Onion Crostini
with Asiago Shavings

1	**baguette**	
½ cup	**olive oil** *(approx.)*	**125 ml**
1 clove	**garlic,** *sliced*	
2	**medium red onions**	
	salt and freshly ground black pepper	
1 tbsp	**balsamic vinegar**	**15 ml**
1 tsp	**thyme**	**5 ml**
16–20	**shavings of Asiago cheese**	

TIPS:

• The onions can be prepared ahead and kept in a covered container in the refrigerator for 1–2 days. The crostini are best made the day of serving.

• A swivel-bladed potato peeler is the perfect tool to make fine shavings of hard cheeses such as Asiago.

• You can caramelize the onions on the stove: Slice thinly and cook slowly over medium-low heat in 2 tbsp (30 ml) of olive oil, stirring now and again, until onions are soft and well browned. Proceed as above.

• *Homemade Italian-style crostini – small slices of toasted bread with a savoury topping (from the Italian for "little crust") – form the base of many wonderful snacks and appetizers. Here, they are topped with sweet, meltingly soft red onions and a sliver of sharp cheese.*

1. Cut baguette into ½" (1 cm) slices on the diagonal. Let garlic sit in ¼ cup (60 ml) of the olive oil for about 15 minutes, then brush each slice lightly on both sides with the flavoured oil.

2. Place bread slices on baking trays and bake at 400°F (200°C) for about 10 minutes, turning once. Or grill the slices on the barbecue until they are nicely marked on both sides. Set aside.

3. Peel onions and slice into ½" (1 cm) rounds. Spear horizontally through the slices with 2 toothpicks or a bamboo skewer to keep the rings together. Brush each slice with olive oil and season with a little salt and pepper.

4. Grill slowly over medium heat, turning now and again, until evenly browned and very soft, about 15 minutes. Remove the toothpicks or skewers and toss the grilled onion rings with a splash of balsamic vinegar and the thyme. If the rings are too large, chop them into manageable pieces.

5. At serving time, pile a spoonful of warm or room-temperature caramelized onions on each of the crostini and top each with a shaving of Asiago cheese.

Makes 16–20 crostini.

Better-than-Bought Hummus
and a Trio of Variations

1½ cups	cooked chickpeas,	375 ml
	rinsed and drained	
	(19 oz/540 ml can)	
2 cloves	garlic, chopped	
1 tbsp	olive oil	15 ml
3 tbsp	fresh lemon juice	45 ml
¼ cup	tahini	60 ml
1 tsp	salt	5 ml
2–3 tbsp	water	30-45 ml
½ tsp	cayenne	2 ml

VARIATIONS:

• **Red Pepper Hummus:** Roast or grill one red pepper. Remove blackened skin and seeds. Add to above mixture and blend until smooth.

• **Roasted Garlic Hummus:** Omit fresh garlic. Add 4–6 cloves of freshly roasted garlic (p. 50) and blend until smooth.

• **Fresh Herb Hummus:** Add 1 tsp (5 ml) cumin and ¼ cup (60 ml) each fresh chopped coriander and mint or Italian (flat-leaf) parsley.

• *You can find ready-made versions of this popular Middle Eastern chickpea dip in the supermarket. But when you need a quick munchie, it's very easy to make your own – especially if you keep a can of chickpeas and a jar of tahini in the cupboard. You'll find the fresh flavour of homemade hummus far superior to the storebought version. Serve with wedges of warm pita bread, Moroccan olives, and slices of fresh lemon.*

1. In a blender or food processor blend together garlic, oil, lemon juice, tahini, salt, water, and cayenne.

2. Shake the chickpeas in a sieve and quickly pick out as many of the tough little skins as are easily removed. Add the chickpeas to the garlic mixture and blend until smooth. (Or mash all the ingredients together by hand.)

3. Taste and add more salt and/or lemon juice if necessary. Add a little more water if mixture is too thick. (It will thicken as it sits.)

4. Spoon the hummus into a shallow bowl, make an indentation in the centre and add a spoonful of flavourful olive oil.

Makes 2 cups (500 ml).

TIP:

• Tahini, a paste made from crushed sesame seeds, is an ingredient in many Middle Eastern dishes. It's readily available nowadays in large supermarkets (in jars) and in bulk-food stores (where it's sold like bulk peanut butter).

(Better-than-Bought Hummus is shown in the photo opposite the next page.)

Pesto Duo
Roasted Pepper Pesto & Sun-Dried Tomato Pesto

Roasted Pepper Pesto

4	roasted peppers, 2 yellow, 2 red	
1 clove	garlic, *minced*	
¼ cup	red onion, *finely minced*	60 ml
1 tsp	balsamic vinegar	5 ml
2 tbsp	fresh parsley, *finely chopped*	30 ml
1 tbsp	fresh basil, *finely chopped*	15 ml
1 tsp	extra-virgin olive oil	5 ml

Sun-Dried Tomato Pesto

1 cup	sun-dried tomatoes in oil	250 ml
¼ cup	blanched almonds	60 ml
1 clove	garlic	
1 strip	lemon zest	
½ cup	fresh basil	125 ml
¼ cup	fresh parsley	60 ml
⅓ cup	extra-virgin olive oil	75 ml

• *These two spreads are quick to make and extremely versatile. Serve them as is accompanied by slices of toasted baguette, plain bagel crisps, or whole-wheat crispbread. Or spoon the pesto on top of creamy goat cheese or deli-style cream cheese, and let guests spread a little of each on baguette toasts or crispbread. The pestos are also delicious tossed with pasta for a quick dinner.*

Roasted Pepper Pesto

1. Peel and chop peppers. Combine with remaining ingredients. Add salt and freshly ground black pepper to taste. *Makes about 1½ cups (375 ml).*

Sun-Dried Tomato Pesto

1. Combine tomatoes, almonds, garlic, lemon zest, and herbs in the bowl of a food processor. Pulse until mixture is evenly chopped.

2. Add half the olive oil and pulse to combine. Add remaining oil and pulse again until mixture is a paste but with some texture remaining. Season to taste. *Makes about 1 cup (250 ml).*

TIPS:

• The spreads can be prepared ahead and stored in the refrigerator for about 3–5 days.

• You can substitute 1 tbsp (15 ml) fresh lemon juice for the balsamic vinegar in the pepper pesto.

Front to back: Sun-Dried Tomato Pesto, Better-than-Bought Hummus (p. 13), and Roasted Pepper Pesto. The pestos are also delicious over creamy goat cheese.

Cottage Tapenade

1 cup	black olives, *pitted*	250 ml
1 cup	pimento-stuffed green olives	250 ml
1 clove	garlic	
¼ cup	fresh parsley	60 ml
1 tbsp	red wine vinegar	15 ml
1 tsp	fresh lemon juice	5 ml
¼ cup	extra-virgin olive oil	60 ml
	salt and freshly ground black pepper	

TIPS:

• The tapenade can be made ahead and stored in the fridge for 3–5 days.

• If you don't have a food processor, finely chop the ingredients by hand.

• *Although prepared tapenade is available, you can quickly and easily make your own version of this Mediterranean olive spread. Serve with garlic toasts, or spread on grilled slices of crusty bread to make bruschetta.*

1. Combine olives, garlic, parsley, vinegar, and lemon juice in the bowl of a food processor. Pulse until mixture is evenly chopped.

2. Add half the olive oil and pulse to combine. Add remaining oil and pulse again until mixture is a fine paste but with some texture remaining.

Makes about 1 cup (250 ml).

QUICK TRICK:

Cheater's Devilish Cheese Twists: Start with store-bought puff pastry instead of making your own pastry. Roll the puff pastry out to a thickness of about ⅛" (3 mm), sprinkle half of it with grated Cheddar and Parmesan cheese and a pinch or two of cayenne, and fold over the other half. Roll again to a thickness of about ⅛" (3 mm). Following directions on facing page, cut into strips and twist, brush with egg wash, and sprinkle with toppings as desired. Bake in preheated 400°F (200°C) oven for 10–15 minutes until twists are golden-brown. Serve warm.

Devilish Cheese Twists

2 cups	flour	500 ml
½ tsp	salt	2 ml
½ tsp	cayenne	2 ml
½ cup	cold butter, *cut in chunks*	125 ml
3 cups	old Cheddar cheese, *grated*	750 ml
¼ cup	Parmesan cheese, *grated*	60 ml
4–5 tbsp	cold water	60–75 ml
1	egg	
	coarse sea salt, sesame seeds, poppy seeds, *and/or* additional cheese *(for topping)*	

TIPS:

• The pastry can be made several days ahead and kept, well wrapped, in the refrigerator.

• The baked cheese twists can be frozen; reheat in a hot oven just before serving.

• *You won't believe how quickly these spicy, melt-in-the-mouth twists will disappear at cocktail hour. The pastry is quick and easy to make – especially with a food processor, but a good old pastry blender will also do the job.*

1. Combine flour, salt, and cayenne in food processor, add butter, and pulse machine on and off until mixture forms coarse crumbs. Add both cheeses to mixture, using same on/off technique.

2. Gradually sprinkle 4 tbsp (60 ml) of ice-cold water over mixture and pulse until pastry comes together. If it isn't holding together, add 1 tbsp (15 ml) more water. Do not overprocess.

3. On a lightly floured surface roll out pastry until it's about ⅛" (3 mm) thick. Cut into strips about ½" (1 cm) wide and 6" (15 cm) long. Twist each strip once or twice, and place on greased and floured or parchment-lined baking sheets.

4. Beat egg lightly with 1 tbsp (15 ml) water and brush twists with the egg wash. Sprinkle with the toppings as desired.

5. Bake in preheated 400°F (200°C) oven for 10–15 minutes until cheese twists are golden-brown. Cool on racks.

Makes about 30 twists.

(Devilish Cheese Twists are shown in the photo opposite p. 120.)

Mussels on the Half Shell
with Roasted Tomato Corn Salsa

24	large mussels	
1 cup	dry white wine	250 ml
¼ cup	shallots *or* onion, *finely chopped*	60 ml
2–3 cloves	garlic, *finely chopped*	
1 tbsp	olive oil	15 ml
1	small bay leaf	
2–3 sprigs	coriander *or* parsley	
pinch	red pepper flakes	
	freshly ground black pepper	
½ cup	Roasted Tomato Corn Salsa *(p. 20)*	125 ml

VARIATIONS:

• The mussels can be served, steaming hot from the pan, in deep bowls with some of the cooking broth, freshly ground pepper, a garnish of chopped fresh parsley, and a loaf of warm crusty bread to mop up the good juices.

• *There was a time when preparing mussels for cooking was quite a chore. Now, however, you can buy wonderful cultivated mussels, which are raised in controlled conditions and usually so clean they only require a quick rinse – no scrubbing or soaking. Here, the mussels are steamed in a fragrant wine broth and used to create a colourful eat-out-of-your-hand appetizer.*

1. Clean mussels thoroughly, trimming away beards if necessary.

2. In a large frying pan, combine wine, shallots or onion, garlic, olive oil, herbs, and spices. Bring to a boil and simmer for 2–3 minutes.

3. Add mussels to the pan, cover and boil for 5 minutes, shaking the pan occasionally so the mussels cook evenly. Remove open mussels to a platter with tongs. Replace lid and cook any unopened mussels for a minute or two longer. Discard any that stubbornly refuse to open.

4. Discard the top shells of the mussels, season lightly, and top each one with a spoonful of Roasted Tomato Corn Salsa.

Makes 24.

TIPS:

• The appetizers can be prepared a few hours ahead, wrapped in plastic, and refrigerated until serving.

• Be sure to purchase your mussels at a market where you can rely on freshness. Mussels must be alive and have their shells clamped shut; discard any that are open or have cracked shells. Keep refrigerated and prepare on the day of purchase.

Mussels steamed in a fragrant wine broth are delicious on their own – but top them with Roasted Tomato Corn Salsa and they become a spectacular appetizer.

Roasted Tomato Corn Salsa

1	**fresh ear of corn,** *husk and silk removed*	
6	**plum tomatoes**	
1 tbsp	**olive oil**	15 ml
¼ cup	**red onion,** *finely chopped*	60 ml
¼ cup	**fresh or roasted red pepper,** *finely chopped*	60 ml
½	**jalapeño pepper,** *seeded and finely chopped*	
2 tbsp	**fresh coriander,** *chopped*	30 ml
1 tbsp	**lime juice**	15 ml
	salt and freshly ground black pepper	

TIP:

• You can make the salsa 2–3 days ahead (keep it refrigerated), but add the coriander on the day of serving.

• Not just a topping for mussels (p. 18). Serve it in a bowl to be scooped up with tortilla chips, or alongside fried fish (p. 145) or grilled chicken. Save time and cut down on last-minute preparation by cooking the vegetables a night or two ahead, while you have the barbecue on for supper.

1. Blanch corn for 2 minutes in boiling salted water. Drain.

2. Rub corn and tomatoes with olive oil and set on the grill over medium-high heat. Roll the corn over the fire for 3–4 minutes until it is nicely browned. Scrape off the kernels.

3. Continue to grill the tomatoes for another few minutes until they are soft and the skins are nicely charred. Chop coarsely.

4. Combine the ingredients and let stand at least an hour for flavours to blend. Adjust seasoning to taste.

Makes 1½ cups (375 ml).

QUICK TRICK:

Lemon Marinated Mussels also make a great appetizer: Steam mussels as described on p. 18. Discard shells. Prepare a vinaigrette by whisking together ¼ cup (60 ml) olive oil, 1 tbsp (15 ml) lemon juice, salt, and freshly ground pepper. Toss mussels with the vinaigrette and add 1 tsp (5 ml) grated lemon zest, 2 finely chopped green onions, and ¼ cup (60 ml) freshly chopped parsley. Serve with hot grilled garlic bread as part of an antipasto selection.

Nuts for Nibbling
Tamari Almonds and Toasted Rosemary Walnuts

Tamari Almonds

1 tbsp	olive oil	15 ml
1 tsp	garlic, *chopped*	5 ml
1 tsp	fresh ginger, *chopped*	5 ml
1 tbsp	soy sauce	15 ml
2 cups	blanched almonds	500 ml
1 tsp	Chinese five-spice powder *(optional)*	5 ml
1 tsp	kosher *or* sea salt	5 ml

Rosemary Walnuts

1 tbsp	olive oil	15 ml
1 tbsp	butter	15 ml
1 strip	lemon zest	
2 tbsp	fresh rosemary, *finely chopped* or	30 ml
1 tbsp	dried rosemary	15 ml
2 cups	walnut halves	500 ml
1 tsp	kosher *or* sea salt	5 ml

TIP:

• The nuts can be stored in covered jars for a week or two, but you may need to crisp them for a few minutes in the oven before serving.

• *Consider doubling the recipes; these savoury snacks never last long. They're particularly good served warm from the oven.*

Tamari Almonds

1. Combine oil, garlic, ginger, and soy sauce and set aside for 30 minutes for flavours to blend. Strain.

2. Heat flavoured oil in a large, heavy frying pan. Add almonds, five-spice powder (optional), and salt. Toss over medium heat for a minute until nuts are evenly coated.

3. Spread on a baking sheet in a single layer and toast in a 300°F (150°C) oven for 20–30 minutes, stirring occasionally. Check often – the window between perfect golden nuts and burned ones is small. Turn nuts out on a rack lined with paper towel to cool a bit before serving.

Toasted Rosemary Walnuts

1. Heat oil, butter, lemon zest, and rosemary in a large heavy skillet. Add walnuts and salt and toss for about a minute until nuts are evenly coated. Discard lemon zest.

2. Spread walnuts on a baking sheet in a single layer and proceed as above.

Each recipe makes 2 cups (500 ml).

(Toasted Rosemary Walnuts are shown in the photo on p. 10.)

Easy Thai-Style Shrimp Rolls

½ lb	**shrimp,** *cooked and chopped*	250 g
½ cup	**bean sprouts**	125 ml
½ cup	**carrot,** *grated*	125 ml
¼ cup	**water chestnuts,** *rinsed, drained, and chopped*	60 ml
3	**green onions,** *finely chopped*	
¼ cup	**fresh coriander,** *chopped*	60 ml
2 tbsp	**Peanut Dipping Sauce** *(following page)*	30 ml
10–12	**round rice-paper wrappers**	

TIP:

• The filling is flexible, and could include other vegetables, such as finely shredded napa cabbage, grated celery, or finely slivered mushrooms. You could also include a little fresh chopped mint and basil in the mix if you have them. (Substituting dried herbs in this recipe is not recommended.)

• *These rice-paper-wrapped parcels are a simplified version of a popular Thai snack. Crisp, fresh, healthy, and fun to eat, they're guaranteed to be a hit. And they can be made ahead, requiring no work at the last minute. The dried rice-paper wrappers are now found in the oriental food section of many supermarkets and will keep for months in the cupboard, ready to make tasty little bites.*

1. Combine shrimp with vegetables, herbs, and Peanut Dipping Sauce. Season to taste.

2. To assemble the shrimp rolls: Have a bowl of hot water beside you and spread out a clean tea towel on your counter. One at a time, dip the rice-paper wrappers in water for 10 seconds, then place on the towel. Place about 2–3 tbsp (30–45 ml) of filling in a small log shape across the middle third of the wrapper. Fold the bottom third of the wrapper over the filling, then turn in each side. Dip your finger in water and lightly moisten the rim of the upper part of the wrapper and roll it up.

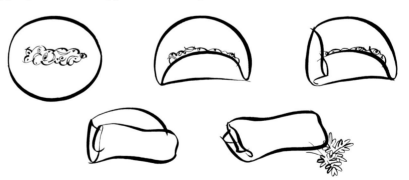

Please turn to next page

Thai-Style Shrimp Rolls: A little practice may be required to get the hang of working with the rice-paper wrappers, but it's worth it. These are a real hit.

Easy Thai-Style Shrimp Rolls, *continued*

3. Place the assembled shrimp rolls seam side down on a baking sheet, cover securely with plastic wrap, and set in the refrigerator until serving. Serve with Peanut Dipping Sauce or the light variation, below.

Makes 10–12.

Peanut Dipping Sauce

1. Combine ingredients thoroughly. Add warm water a spoonful at a time to obtain a light creamy texture. Taste and adjust seasoning with added lime juice or salt.

Makes about 1 cup (250 ml).

VARIATION:

• For a light alternate dipping sauce, combine 2 tbsp (30 ml) each of soy sauce and rice vinegar, 1 tsp (5 ml) roasted sesame oil, a little sugar, and a finely chopped green onion.

Peanut Dipping Sauce

½ cup	natural chunky peanut butter	125 ml
2 tbsp	rice vinegar	30 ml
2 tbsp	fresh lime juice	30 ml
2 tbsp	soy sauce	30 ml
2 tsp	brown sugar	10 ml
2 cloves	garlic, *finely chopped*	
½ tsp	chili paste or	2 ml
pinch	dried chili flakes	

TIPS:

• The rolls can be prepared several hours before serving and refrigerated.

• At an informal gathering, get guests involved in making the rolls. (Producing a neat, easy-to-eat roll without tearing the rice paper takes some practice, so count on a few imperfect rolls being devoured in the kitchen along the way.)

• As a time-saver, buy small precooked "salad" shrimp. Since you're chopping them anyway, there's no need to spend more on larger sizes.

Baked Brie
with Cranberry Relish & Toasted Pecans

1	**8 oz whole brie** or **Camembert**, *chilled*	**250 g**
½ cup	**cranberry relish**	**125 ml**
1 tbsp	**orange zest,** *grated*	**15 ml**
1 cup	**pecan halves,** *toasted*	**250 ml**

TIPS:

• The brie can be placed on a sheet of foil and baked in the barbecue over medium heat for about 15 minutes.

• For how to toast the pecan halves, see p. 155.

VARIATION:

• Top the brie with Sun-Dried Tomato Pesto (p. 14) or Roasted Pepper Pesto (p. 14) and bake as above. Serve with toasted almonds and baguette rounds.

• *There are numerous variations on the baked brie theme, but I particularly like the look and tart-sweet taste of this one. With a jar of good cranberry relish (with whole cranberries) and a small whole brie on hand, you can put this together in minutes. Serve with toasted baguette rounds or small triangles of toasted egg bread.*

1. Place cheese wheel in a shallow ovenproof dish. Lightly prick top surface of the cheese and spread with an even layer of cranberry relish.

2. Bake in a preheated 400°F (200°C) oven for 10–15 minutes, until cheese just starts to bulge around the edges and the centre is soft.

3. Sprinkle grated orange zest on top and surround with toasted pecans. Serve warm.

Makes about 8 servings.

QUICK TRICK:

When time is tight, take advantage of the excellent prepared foods available in supermarkets and specialty stores, but dress them up with a simple touch or two of your own: For example, serve a ready-made chicken-liver pâté with thin slices of crisp green apple and assorted crackers, or a mild, creamy blue cheese with slices of firm ripe pear, walnut halves, and oatmeal biscuits. Or top creamy goat cheese or cream cheese with a ready-made pesto and serve with toasted baguette rounds.

(The Baked Brie with Cranberry Relish & Toasted Pecans is shown in the photo on the following page.)

Grilled Eggplant Rounds
with Artichoke & Feta Topping

1–2	medium eggplants	
	olive oil	
1 cup	salsa *or* sliced tomatoes	250 ml
1 cup	feta cheese, *crumbled*	250 ml
1 jar	marinated artichoke hearts, *chopped* *(6 oz/170 ml)*	
2 tbsp	fresh basil, *chopped*	30 ml
	salt and freshly ground black pepper	

TIP:

• Also delicious as a side dish with grilled chicken, steak, or pork chops, or as a topping to dress up grilled burgers.

• *This done-on-the-barbecue appetizer requires just a few minutes to prepare. For a bite-sized version, use slender oriental eggplant and plum tomatoes.*

1. Cut eggplant into ³⁄₈" (1 cm) slices. Brush both sides of slices with olive oil.

2. Grill on barbecue over medium heat for a few minutes on each side until eggplant is almost tender.

3. With eggplant still on barbecue, top each piece with a tomato slice or salsa, and sprinkle cheese on top. Scatter chopped artichoke and basil over cheese. Season to taste with salt and pepper. Heat until warmed through.

Makes 12–15 slices.

QUICK TRICK:

Bocconcini Bites: Bocconcini – small fresh mozzarella balls – are available at the cheese or deli counter of many supermarkets. For an instant hors d'oeuvre, slice them and toss with olive oil, pepper, salt, and herbs. Serve on a plate with strips of sun-dried tomato, curls of prosciutto, ripe olives, and some good crusty bread. Or top crostini (p. 12) with a slice or two of bocconcini and strips of roasted peppers.

Left, a new twist on an old theme: Baked Brie with Cranberry Relish and Toasted Pecans (recipe on previous page). Above: Grilled Eggplant Rounds.

Portobellos on Polenta Circles

2 cups	cornmeal	500 ml
6 cups	water	1.5 L
1½ tsp	salt	7 ml
2–4 tbsp	butter *(optional)*	30–60 ml
	Portobello Mushroom Topping *(facing page)*	

QUICK TRICKS:

Packages of instant cornmeal, imported from Italy, are a terrific shortcut, requiring only 5 minutes to prepare, and they make excellent polenta. (Beretta is one brand.) Follow the cooking directions on the package.

• Quicker still: In some markets you will find premade polenta in a sausage-shaped roll, which is ready to use, right out of the package. Cut the roll into ⅜" (1 cm) slices, brush each side of the circles with olive oil, and grill as above.

• *Polenta, a kind of cornmeal porridge, is as popular in northern Italy as pasta is in southern, and is frequently served hot as a side dish. It can also be cooled, sliced, browned on the grill, and used as a tasty base for a variety of appetizer toppings – such as grilled portobello mushrooms. Instant and ready-made polenta (see Quick Tricks, left) can shorten the prep time dramatically.*

1. Bring water and salt to a boil in a large deep pot. Add cornmeal in a slow steady stream, whisking vigorously to avoid lumps.

2. Lower the heat and stir, almost constantly, until cornmeal is cooked, about 30 minutes. (The polenta is done when it becomes smooth and pulls away from the sides of the pot.) Stir in butter if desired.

3. Spread the cooked polenta in a smooth, even layer about ⅜" (1 cm) thick on baking sheets. Cover with plastic wrap and leave to cool.

4. Using a cookie cutter or glass, cut polenta into small circles. Brush on both sides with a little olive oil and grill over medium heat until nicely marked and hot.

5. Place a spoonful of Portobello Mushroom Topping on each piece of polenta. Serve hot.

Makes about 20 appetizer pieces.

TIP:

• The polenta can be made ahead and kept in the refrigerator for 1–2 days.

Topping

6	**portobello mushrooms,** *stems removed*	
½ cup	**extra-virgin olive oil**	**125 ml**
2 cloves	**garlic,** *finely chopped*	
2 tbsp	**balsamic vinegar**	**30 ml**
½ cup	**Italian (flat-leaf) parsley,** *finely chopped*	**125 ml**
	salt and freshly ground black pepper	

VARIATIONS:

• Top the grilled polenta circles with Caramelized Red Onions and Asiago (p. 12) or a spoonful of your favourite salsa. (The flavour of the Roasted Tomato Corn Salsa – p. 20 – works particularly well with the grilled polenta.) Or try the Simple Tomato Salad (Quick Trick, p. 82) on top; just chop the tomato wedges into smaller pieces.

Portobello Mushroom Topping

Portobellos – a big brown variety of the common mushroom – have a wonderful meaty texture and great flavour. Grilled, then tossed with a little balsamic vinegar, they make a splendid appetizer piled on polenta circles or grilled Italian-style bread.

1. Clean mushroom caps carefully so as not to damage them.

2. Combine oil and garlic. Brush mushroom caps with flavoured oil on both sides. Set aside for an hour or so.

3. Preheat the barbecue and lightly oil the rack. Grill the mushrooms over medium heat for 5–7 minutes a side until tender and nicely browned.

4. Remove from heat, slice into narrow strips, and toss with balsamic vinegar, parsley and seasoning. (If mushrooms are large, cut strips in half.) Pile warm portobellos onto grilled polenta circles and serve at once.

Makes about 2 cups (500 ml), or topping for 20 polenta circles.

TIP:

• Portobello stems are tougher than the tops, but still flavourful. Cut off the earthy end and discard. Rinse the stem, then chop or thinly slice and add to soups or stews.

Cottage Canoes

12	**large jalapeño peppers**	
1½ cups	**old Cheddar cheese,** *finely shredded*	**375 ml**
¼ cup	**mayonnaise**	**60 ml**
1	**green onion,** *finely chopped*	
1 stalk	**celery,** *finely chopped*	
½ tsp	**Worcestershire sauce**	**2 ml**
1	**egg,** *beaten*	
1 cup	**seasoned dry bread crumbs**	**250 ml**

TIPS:

• Leave the stems on the peppers. They make a nice handle for easy dipping and eating.

• If your skin is sensitive, wear rubber gloves while handling the peppers.

• *This spicy appetizer got its name because the pepper halves look like the ubiquitous green canoes you see all over Ontario's cottage country.*

1. Cut peppers in half lengthwise and remove ribs and seeds.

2. Mix cheese, mayonnaise, onion, celery, and Worcestershire sauce. Fill peppers with cheese mixture, pressing down on top to flatten. Chill for 20 minutes.

3. Roll each pepper in beaten egg, then dredge in bread crumbs to coat thoroughly. Place on baking sheet.

4. Bake in preheated 350°F (180°C) oven for 10–12 minutes, or until canoe tops are slightly crisp.

Makes 24 pieces.

QUICK TRICK:

Three-Pepper Chip Dip is the solution when plain potato chips need company and onion dip lacks excitement: Combine 1 cup (250 ml) sour cream, or half sour cream and half yogurt, with ½ cup (125 ml) finely chopped sweet red pepper, 1 tsp (5 ml) finely chopped jalapeño pepper, and 1 tsp (5 ml) chili powder. Add a dash of hot sauce for good measure, and a little salt. Allow the dip to sit a while before serving so the flavours will blend – the longer it sits, the hotter it gets.

Bet you can't stop at one: These Cottage Canoes have real bite, and go extremely well with a glass of cold beer.

Red Pepper & Feta Spread

4	**sweet red peppers,** *roasted, peeled, seeded, and chopped*	
½–1	**fresh hot red pepper,** *seeded and chopped (or to taste)*	
2 cloves	**garlic,** *minced*	
2 tbsp	**extra-virgin olive oil**	30 ml
1 lb	**feta cheese,** *crumbled*	500 g
	freshly ground black pepper	
	squeeze of fresh lemon juice	

TIPS:

• The spread can be made ahead and will keep in the refrigerator for up to three days.

• To convert the spread into a creamy dip to serve with fresh vegetables, stir in 2 tbsp (30 ml) of yogurt after blending in the feta.

• For how to roast peppers, see recipe, p. 120.

• *Delicious on toasted pita triangles at cocktail hour, as a sandwich spread (with grilled lamb on top), or as the base of a wrap stuffed with grilled veggies.*

1. Place peppers, garlic, and olive oil in a food processor and blend to a paste.

2. Add feta cheese and pulse to combine just until smooth. Do not over-process or the cheese will become too runny.

3. Taste and adjust seasoning. Depending on the quality of the feta, you may need to add a squeeze of lemon juice or a few grindings of black pepper. (Since the feta is salty, it's unlikely you'll need additional salt.)

Makes 2 cups (500 ml).

QUICK TRICK:

Combine equal amounts of grated smoked cheddar cheese and Swiss cheese with a few chopped black olives, a splash of vermouth, and a little soft butter. Spread mixture on thin slices of good bread (olive bread is great with this) and set in the toaster oven or under the broiler until the cheese melts. Cut into fingers and serve.

Roast the red peppers and make the spread ahead of time, then serve it at cocktail hour with toasted pita bread and kalamata olives mixed with hot pepper flakes.

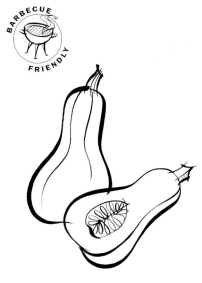

2	butternut squash *(approx. 2 lbs/1 kg)*	
	salt and freshly ground black pepper	
6 tbsp	olive oil	90 ml
1 head	garlic	
3 tbsp	tahini	45 ml
2 tbsp	lemon juice	30 ml
¼ tsp	cayenne	1 ml

TIPS:

• The squash and garlic can be roasted on the barbecue. Toss with olive oil, season, and wrap in foil. Cook with the cover down for about 20 minutes, or until tender.

• The dip can be made 1–2 days ahead and stored, covered, in the refrigerator.

• Tahini, a smooth paste of sesame seeds, is found in most supermarkets, but cream or cream cheese make tasty substitutes.

Roasted Squash & Garlic Dip

• *This variation on the traditional Middle Eastern dip baba ghanouj uses squash instead of eggplant as the main ingredient, and roasted garlic (which is sweeter and milder) instead of raw. Serve with Spicy Pita Wedges (facing page), pita triangles, bread sticks, bagel crisps, or raw vegetables.*

1. Cut, peel, and seed squash and cut into chunks or slice into wedges. Toss with about 2 tbsp (30 ml) olive oil and season with salt and pepper. Spread squash on a baking sheet and roast in a 400°F (200°C) oven for 15 minutes. Turn pieces over and continue to roast until squash is tender and nicely browned on all sides, about 15 minutes longer.

2. Slice about ½" (1 cm) off the top of the head of garlic, wrap head in foil, and roast in the oven with the squash.

3. Squeeze garlic out of skin and blend with roasted squash, tahini, remaining olive oil, and lemon juice in a food processor until smooth. Adjust seasoning with cayenne, salt, and more lemon juice to taste.

Makes 4 cups (1 L).

Spicy Pita Wedges

1 pkg	pita bread	6–8 rounds
½ cup	olive oil	125 ml
¼ tsp	cayenne *or* **a few shakes of hot sauce**	1 ml
2–3 cloves	garlic, *minced*	

TIP:

• If the pita bread has a pocket, you can make pita crisps: Cut each round into 8 wedges and split the wedges apart. Brush with the seasoned oil and bake in the oven as above.

• *These make great dippers for Roasted Squash & Garlic Dip (facing page), Red Pepper & Feta Spread (p. 32), or Better-than-Bought Hummus (p. 13).*

1. Season olive oil with cayenne and minced garlic and brush on both sides of pita rounds.

2. Grill on a medium-hot barbecue for about 10 minutes, turning once, taking care not to let pitas burn. Alternatively, arrange in a single layer on a baking sheet in a 400°F (200°C) oven and bake until lightly browned, turning once, about 10 minutes.

3. Cut each pita into 8 wedges and serve warm.

Makes 48–64 wedges.

QUICK TRICK:

Smoked salmon is always popular, but for something different, try smoked trout as an easy beginning to a summer meal. Remove skin and bones from the trout and place the fillets on a platter. Garnish with red onion rings, lemon wedges, and fresh dill, and accompany with Grainy Mustard and Dill Sauce (p. 67) or store-bought tzatziki and fresh rye bread or crispbread. If you're feeling ambitious, pickled beets and pickled cucumbers (p. 92) also go well with the trout.

II. GREAT GRILLING

Peppered Sirloin Steak (p. 57) and Lazy Summer Paella (p. 41)

CONTENTS

Many of these recipes can be used with more than one type or cut of meat; suggestions are included either in the introduction to the recipe or in an "Also Great With" or "Tips" section at its end.

QUICK TRICKS

IN OTHER CHAPTERS...

More from the Barbecue

These recipes – located in other sections of the book – also use the barbecue or have an option for barbecue cooking:

CROWD PLEASERS

Sizzling Summer Celebration Dinner (for 6)

Chilled Carrot Ginger Soup *(p. 118)*

Pepper-Encrusted Loin of Pork *(p. 44)*
with grilled pineapple or
Pineapple Salsa *(p. 87)*

**Wheat Berry Salad with Wild Rice
& Orzo** *(p. 72)*

Tossed green salad

Warm breads

Espresso Ice Cream Loaf *(p. 163)* **with
Decadent Fudge Cookies** *(p. 174)*

Vegetarian Entertaining (for 4)

Sun-Dried Tomato Pesto *(p. 14)* with
creamy goat cheese or cream
cheese and toasts

Eggplant & Tomato Salad *(p. 43)*

Grilled Polenta Slices *(p. 28)* with
Portobello Mushroom Topping
(p. 29)

White Bean & Spinach Salad *(p. 80)*

Grilled Mint Julep Peaches *(p. 183)*
with vanilla ice cream

Wine-Marinated Steak Kebabs

2 lbs	sirloin steak	1 kg

Red Wine Marinade

1½ cups	dry red wine	375 ml
½ cup	olive oil	125 ml
¼ cup	red wine vinegar	60 ml
1	onion, *sliced*	
4 cloves	garlic, *chopped*	
2	bay leaves	
1 tbsp	fresh rosemary, *chopped* or	15 ml
1 tsp	dried rosemary	5 ml
	salt and freshly ground black pepper	

TIP:

• Skewer the beef on trimmings from grapevines or the woody twigs of fresh herbs such as rosemary or sage. They provide aromatic smoke and make for an attractive presentation. Soak the vines or twigs in water for an hour and pierce the pieces of meat with a wooden or metal skewer before threading them on.

• *Beef melts in the mouth after a few hours in this gutsy marinade. Serve with Summer Vegetable Kebabs (p. 51) and creamy garlic mashed potatoes.*

1. Trim steak and cut into uniform chunks of about 1½" (4 cm).

2. Combine remaining ingredients and toss the steak in the marinade. Leave for several hours or as long as overnight in a covered dish in the refrigerator.

3. Soak 10" (25 cm) bamboo skewers in water for about an hour.

4. When ready to cook, remove beef from marinade and pat dry. Reserve ¼ cup (60 ml) of the marinade for basting and strain the remainder into a small saucepan. Bring to a boil and simmer for 8–10 minutes to reduce by half and create a sauce. Taste and adjust seasoning.

5. Thread 6 pieces of steak on each skewer, and place on a hot, lightly oiled grill over high heat. Turn and baste with marinade until nicely browned and grilled to your taste – 8–10 minutes for medium rare. Remove from grill. Season with salt and freshly ground pepper and coat with a spoonful of sauce.

Serves 4.

ALSO GREAT WITH:

• Use the marinade for a whole steak and grill as for Peppered Sirloin (p. 57). It's also delicious with lamb – either kebabs, chops, or a whole leg.

Crispy Ginger Garlic Chicken

4 lbs	chicken pieces	2 kg
½ cup	sesame seeds, *toasted*	125 ml
2	green onions, *thinly sliced on the diagonal*	
2 tbsp	fresh coriander, *chopped (optional)*	30 ml

Ginger Garlic Marinade

½ cup	soy sauce	125 ml
¼ cup	fresh lime juice	60 ml
2 tbsp	brown sugar *or* **honey**	30 ml
1 tbsp	vegetable oil	15 ml
1 tbsp	sesame oil	15 ml
2	green onions, *finely chopped*	
2 cloves	garlic, *finely chopped*	
1" piece	fresh ginger, *peeled and minced*	2.5 cm
1 tbsp	hot sauce **or**	15 ml
1 tsp	hot chili flakes	5 ml
1 tbsp	fresh coriander, *chopped (optional)*	15 ml

• Flavourful Asian-style chicken pieces – crisp on the outside, tender and moist on the inside. For a real treat, leave the skin on.

1. Combine marinade ingredients. Pour half the marinade over the chicken, reserving the rest to use as a basting sauce and to serve alongside. Cover the chicken and set aside for an hour or as long as overnight in the refrigerator.

2. Place the chicken pieces on a preheated, lightly oiled grill over a foil drip pan. Cover the barbecue and cook by indirect heat (see p. 9) at a constant medium temperature of about 350°F (180°C) for 30–45 minutes. (Breast pieces will take less time, so check them frequently.) Turn chicken and baste with reserved sauce several times during cooking.

3. Sprinkle with toasted sesame seeds, chopped green onion, and fresh coriander if you like. Serve with remaining reserved marinade alongside.

Serves 6.

TIP:
• The marinade can be made ahead and kept in the refrigerator for several weeks. However, if you're going to keep it longer than overnight, you have to cook it first. Combine ingredients in a small saucepan and simmer for 5 minutes. Strain and store in a covered container.

ALSO GREAT WITH:
• The Ginger Garlic Marinade is delicious with pork or fish, such as tuna, salmon, red snapper, or sea bass. Remember not to marinate fish too long – about 15 minutes is enough – as the acidic ingredients will soften the flesh too much.

Lazy Summer Paella

1½ lbs	large raw shrimp, *peeled and deveined*	675 g
2 tbsp	olive oil	30 ml
squeeze	fresh lemon juice	
2–4 cloves	garlic, *finely chopped*	
1 tsp	dried oregano	5 ml
2–3	chorizo *or* other spicy sausages *(optional)*	
12–24	mussels *and/or* clams *(optional), cleaned*	
	Saffron Rice Pilaf *(p. 95)*	
	lemon slices and fresh parsley, *chopped (for garnish)*	

TIPS:

• The mussels and clams can also be cooked on the barbecue in a grilling basket. Cover and cook for 2–3 minutes until they open.

• Alternatively, steam mussels and clams following the directions on p. 18, and then use the cooking liquid to prepare the rice pilaf.

• *The shrimp are done on skewers on the barbecue and served on top of a fragrant, golden rice pilaf. If you want to be more elaborate (and closer to an authentic paella), you can also grill some spicy sausage and/or steam some fresh mussels or clams to add to the rice.*

1. Combine the olive oil, lemon juice, garlic, and oregano, and toss the shrimp with the mixture. Set aside in the refrigerator for an hour for the shrimp to marinate. Put bamboo skewers in water to soak.

2. Prepare the rice pilaf, following the directions on p. 95. Tuck the mussels and clams (if including) into the rice during the last 5 minutes of cooking time, and continue to cook until they open.

3. Meanwhile, preheat barbecue and lightly oil the grill rack. Prick sausages (if including), brush lightly with oil, and set on preheated grill. Turn to brown evenly and cook thoroughly, about 20 minutes.

4. Thread the shrimp on skewers, and grill over medium-high heat for about 2–3 minutes a side, being careful not to overcook. (Shrimp should be pink on the outside, tender and opaque within.)

5. Fluff the rice with a fork, season, and turn out onto a warm platter. Discard any unopened shellfish. Add the sausages, cut in pieces, and top with skewers of shrimp. Serve at once, garnished with parsley and lemon.

Serves 6.

While the pilaf's cooking, grill the skewered shrimp. If you like, add some mussels to the rice close to the end of the cooking time.

Lemon Rosemary Turkey Breast

1	turkey breast half	
	(3–4 lbs/1.5–2 kg)	
½	lemon	

Lemon Rosemary Marinade

¼ cup	olive oil	60 ml
1 tbsp	fresh rosemary, *chopped*	15 ml
	or	
1 tsp	dried rosemary	5 ml
1 strip	lemon zest	
2 cloves	garlic, *halved*	
	salt and freshly ground black pepper	

TIP:

• For a stronger smoke flavour, add hickory chips to the fire. (See p. 9.)

ALSO GREAT WITH:

• The Lemon Rosemary Marinade is delicious on chicken, too. Try it on boneless breasts.

• *With people looking for more alternatives to red meat, a variety of fresh turkey pieces can now be found in supermarkets year-round. Marinated fresh turkey cooked on the barbecue has a wonderful smoky flavour, and the meat stays nice and moist. If you're lucky, you'll have some left over for sandwiches.*

1. Combine the marinade ingredients and allow to stand for about an hour for flavours to mingle.

2. Rinse the turkey breast under cold running water, then pat dry. Rub all over with the lemon half and season with salt and pepper, then rub all over with the marinade. Refrigerate for a few hours or as long as overnight.

3. Remove turkey from the refrigerator about 30 minutes before cooking. Preheat the barbecue and lightly oil the grill.

4. When the barbecue is ready, place the turkey breast directly on the grill over a drip pan and cover. Cook with indirect heat (see p. 9) for about 1–1½ hours at a temperature of about 325°F (160°C). The turkey breast is done when the juices run clear and the temperature on an instant-read thermometer inserted in the thickest portion registers 170°F (77°C).

5. Remove turkey from grill, and let stand, loosely covered with aluminum foil, for 15–20 minutes before slicing.

Serves 4–6, or 2–4 with plenty left over for sandwiches.

Eggplant & Tomato Salad

2	large eggplants	
4	plum tomatoes, *halved lengthwise*	
2 cloves	garlic, *finely chopped*	
¼ cup	olive oil	60 ml
½	small red onion, *finely sliced*	
½ cup	fresh basil, *finely slivered*	125 ml
2 tbsp	balsamic vinegar	30 ml
	kosher *or* sea salt and freshly ground black pepper	
½ cup	cured black olives *(optional)*	125 ml

● *The barbecue is essential to this salad, as it gives the vegetables a wonderful smoky taste. For an excellent vegetarian meal, partner the salad with grilled polenta wedges with Portobello Mushroom Topping (pp. 28–29).*

1. Cut eggplants into slices about ½" (1 cm) thick. Sprinkle with salt on both sides and set aside for an hour to release the excess liquid. Pat slices dry with paper towel.

2. Combine garlic and olive oil and brush on the eggplant slices and tomato halves.

3. Grill eggplant directly over a medium-hot fire until slices are tender and lightly browned.

4. Grill tomato halves, skin-side down, until skins are nicely charred, then turn over and grill the cut side for a few minutes. Remove and peel off skins, scrape away the seeds, and chop the flesh.

5. Arrange eggplant slices on a platter and top with a layer of chopped grilled tomatoes, onions, and slivered basil. Sprinkle with balsamic vinegar, salt and pepper, and a handful of cured black olives if you like.

6. Cover with plastic wrap and set aside for flavours to develop – an hour at room temperature. Serve at room temperature.

Serves 6.

(Eggplant & Tomato Salad is shown in the photo opposite the next page.)

Pepper-Encrusted Loin of Pork

3½ lb	**pork loin,** *boned*	1.5 kg
¼ cup	**fresh cracked black pepper**	60 ml
2 cloves	**garlic,** *finely chopped*	
1 tsp	**lemon zest,** *grated*	5 ml
1 tsp	**kosher** *or* **sea salt**	5 ml
½ cup	**fresh Italian (flat-leaf) parsley,** *finely chopped*	125 ml
2 tbsp	**olive oil,** *infused with*	30 ml
1 clove	**garlic,** *chopped*	

TIPS:

• The meat can be prepared for the barbecue (through Step 2) ahead of time and kept covered in the refrigerator for up to 8 hours.

• Replace the pepper/herb seasoning inside the pork loin with tapenade (p. 16), Sun-Dried Tomato Pesto (p. 14), or your favourite commercial variation on the pesto theme.

• *Delicious prepared on the barbecue and served, hot or cold, with a selection of condiments: your favourite mustard or homemade chili sauce or, for something a little different, grilled fresh pineapple or Pineapple Salsa (p. 87).*

1. Open out boned pork loin, boned side up. In a small bowl, combine half the cracked black pepper, the garlic, lemon zest, a little salt, and parsley. Sprinkle mixture evenly over the pork. Roll up the roast and tie in several places to form a compact cylinder.

2. Brush the outside of the pork with a little garlic-infused oil and coat with the remaining pepper and a little salt.

3. Preheat the barbecue, then set the meat on the rack over a foil drip pan; close cover and cook, using indirect heat (see p. 9), at a constant medium temperature (about 350°F/180°C). Baste the meat occasionally with the garlic-infused oil.

4. Cooking time will be approximately 1½ hours, but check with an instant-read thermometer after about an hour. The pork is done when the temperature is 160°F (70°C).

5. Remove meat to a warm serving platter, and let rest a few minutes before slicing. Serve accompanied by Pineapple Salsa or grilled pineapple.

Serves 6.

Pepper-Encrusted Loin of Pork (this page) with Pineapple Salsa (in pepper cups; p. 87); also shown: Smoking Red-Hot Ribs (p. 46), Eggplant & Tomato Salad (p. 43).

Smoking Red-Hot Ribs

6 lbs	meaty pork back ribs	3 kg
2 tbsp	vegetable oil	30 ml
	Southern-Style Spicy Barbecue Rub *(below)*	
3 cloves	**garlic,** *finely chopped*	
	Red Hot Barbecue Sauce *(facing page)*	

Barbecue Rub

2 tbsp	chili powder	30 ml
1 tsp	paprika	5 ml
1 tsp	cumin, *ground*	5 ml
1 tsp	cayenne	5 ml
1 tsp	kosher *or* sea salt	5 ml
1 tbsp	freshly ground black pepper	15 ml
1 tbsp	dried oregano	15 ml
1 tbsp	dried thyme	15 ml
1 tbsp	brown sugar	15 ml

• *For a double hit of flavour, the ribs are first coated with Southern-Style Spicy Barbecue Rub, then brushed with Red-Hot Barbecue Sauce near the end of their time on the grill.*

1. Combine all ingredients for barbecue rub.

2. Cut ribs into slabs of about 8 ribs apiece and rub with oil. Then coat them all over with barbecue rub and garlic. Cover and set aside for at least an hour or as long as overnight in the refrigerator.

3. Prepare the barbecue for low, indirect cooking. (See p. 9.) Place the ribs over a foil drip pan. Cover the grill and cook by indirect heat, at a constant low temperature of about 240°F (115°C) for 45 minutes. Turn ribs over and cook for another 1–1½ hours or so, maintaining constant low heat.

4. During the last 20 minutes of cooking, brush ribs with Red-Hot Barbecue Sauce, turning them several times. Serve hot, with extra sauce on the side.

Serves 4–6.

TIP:

• For convenience, you can slow-roast the ribs in the oven ahead of time, then finish them briefly on the barbecue. Roast at 200°F (95°C) for about 3 hours; refrigerate until needed. When you're ready to serve them, return the ribs to room temperature, then set on a clean, lightly oiled grill over medium-high direct heat; sear on each side for a few minutes. Close the lid and continue to cook for about 30 minutes, turning and basting with sauce several times.

(Smoking Red-Hot Ribs are shown in the photo on the previous page.)

Red-Hot Barbecue Sauce

1 tbsp	vegetable oil	15 ml
1	medium onion, *finely chopped*	
2 cloves	garlic, *finely chopped*	
1 can	tomato sauce *(28 oz/796 ml)*	
½ cup	cider vinegar	125 ml
¼ cup	dark brown sugar	60 ml
1 tbsp	molasses	15 ml
½ cup	orange juice	125 ml
1 tsp	paprika	5 ml
2 tsp	chili powder	10 ml
1 tsp	dry mustard	5 ml
	salt and freshly ground black pepper	
½–1	chipotle chili in adobo sauce, *chopped* or hot sauce *(to taste)*	

• *The secret to fantastic ribs! The sauce can be prepared ahead – it will keep about 3–4 weeks in the refrigerator – and is also delicious on grilled pork or chicken. (Try it on wings.)*

1. Heat oil in a large pot over medium heat. Add onion and cook until soft and lightly browned. Add garlic and cook for a minute.

2. Stir in remaining ingredients. Bring to a boil, lower heat, and simmer, uncovered, for an hour or so.

3. Using a blender or food processor, purée the sauce in batches or, if you like it very smooth, press it through a sieve. Store in a covered container in the refrigerator.

Makes 2 cups (500 ml).

TIP:

• **Chipotles are smoked jalapeño peppers, sold dried as well as canned in adobo sauce (a rich tomato sauce). They add a smoky, sweet flavour along with their heat. Look for them in specialty stores or in the Mexican food section of large supermarkets.**

Grilled Fish with Parsley Caper Sauce

2 lbs	fresh fish fillets	1 kg
2 tbsp	melted butter *or* vegetable oil	30 ml
2 tbsp	lemon juice	30 ml
	salt and freshly ground black pepper	

Parsley Caper Sauce

¼ cup	fresh parsley, *chopped*	60 ml
2 tbsp	small capers, *drained and rinsed*	30 ml
1 tbsp	green onion, *minced*	15 ml
1 tsp	lemon zest, *grated*	5 ml
2 tbsp	white wine vinegar	30 ml
1 tbsp	fresh lemon juice	15 ml
⅓ cup	extra-virgin olive oil	75 ml
	salt and freshly ground black pepper	

TIP:

• If the family angler delivers small bass or perch, you may need to use a fish-grilling basket. Or cook the fillets in a frying pan on the stove instead.

• *Freshly caught (or bought) fillets of trout, bass, salmon, or halibut work well in this dish. Serve with Grilled Asparagus (p. 50) and tiny new potatoes, steamed with chopped fresh dill until just tender.*

1. Combine melted butter or oil, lemon juice, and seasoning. Brush mixture lightly over fish fillets.

2. Lay fish on a lightly oiled grill over medium heat and cook for 4–5 minutes for ¼"–½" (0.5–1 cm) fillets. For thicker fillets (½"–1"/1–2.5 cm), turn carefully and continue cooking until the fish is opaque and flakes easily when tested with a fork, about another 4 minutes. (Timing will depend on the thickness of the fillets.)

3. Remove to a platter. Drizzle with Parsley Caper Sauce and serve with additional sauce on the side. Serve hot or at room temperature.

Serves 4.

Parsley Caper Sauce

1. Combine ingredients for sauce. Set aside, covered, in the refrigerator for an hour or so to allow the flavours to meld. Adjust seasoning to taste.

Makes about ¾ cup (175 ml).

The simplicity of Grilled Asparagus (p. 50) and steamed new potatoes makes them good accompaniments to the Grilled Fish with tangy Parsley Caper Sauce.

Grilled Asparagus

2 lbs	fresh asparagus	1 kg
2 tbsp	olive oil	30 ml
dash	lemon juice	
	or **balsamic vinegar**	
	salt and freshly ground black pepper	

QUICK TRICK:

When the barbecue is going, wrap a whole head of garlic in foil and throw it on to roast: Slice horizontally across the top of the head about ½" (1 cm) down from the top, exposing the end of each clove. Rub outside with olive oil. Wrap in foil and place on the grill over medium-high heat, turning occasionally, for about 45 minutes or until soft. Squeeze the cloves out of their skins and:

• add to mashed potatoes

• combine with mayonnaise, for an excellent sandwich spread

• serve as part of a grilled-vegetable side dish or antipasto

• add to the dressing for Roasted Vegetable Pasta Salad (p. 78)

• use as a topping for pizza or focaccia

• spread on crostini (p. 12)

• *Serve the grilled spears with dinner, or tossed with a balsamic vinaigrette as part of an antipasto platter. They're also good accompanied by any of the sauces on p. 67 or a simple mix of melted butter and lemon for dipping.*

1. Trim and wash asparagus and toss into a large pot of boiling, lightly salted water. Cook for about 2 minutes. Drain and plunge into ice water to stop the cooking process. Drain well.

2. Toss asparagus in a shallow dish with olive oil and season with salt and pepper.

3. Lay the spears on the grill over medium-high heat for 2–3 minutes until nicely marked and just tender.

4. Remove from heat, sprinkle with lemon juice or balsamic vinegar, and serve hot or at room temperature.

Serves 6.

(Grilled Asparagus are shown in the photo on the previous page.)

Summer Vegetable Kebabs

1	red pepper	
1	yellow pepper	
2	small Asian eggplant *or* zucchini	
8	small mushrooms	
1	small red onion	
1/3 cup	olive oil	75 ml
2 cloves	garlic, *finely chopped*	
1 tbsp	fresh rosemary, *finely chopped*	15 ml
	or	
1 tsp	dried rosemary	5 ml
	salt and freshly ground black pepper	
1 tbsp	balsamic vinegar	15 ml

TIPS:

• Substitute other vegetables to take advantage of what you find in the market, such as chunks of corn on the cob, whole shallots, or fat asparagus spears.

• Vary the herbs to complement the main dish you're serving, replacing the rosemary with thyme, basil, or oregano. Sprinkle grilled vegetables with more fresh chopped herbs if they are available.

• *Colourful vegetable skewers make attractive individual side dishes to serve with grilled meats. As a serving alternative, you can push the vegetables off the skewers into a bowl after grilling and toss with a splash of balsamic vinegar.*

1. Soak 8 grapevine trimmings, rosemary stalks (see Tip, p. 38), or 10" (25 cm) bamboo skewers in water for about an hour.

2. Halve and seed peppers and cut in uniform chunks. Cut eggplant or zucchini in 1 1/2" (4 cm) rounds. Trim and clean mushrooms. Peel onion, leaving root end intact, and cut lengthwise into even sections.

3. In a large bowl, toss vegetables with oil, garlic, herbs, and seasonings. Thread in a colourful sequence onto prepared skewers.

4. Place vegetable kebabs on a clean, hot, lightly oiled grill over high heat. Turn frequently and baste with any flavoured oil remaining in the bowl until vegetables are lightly charred on the outside and just tender inside – about 10–12 minutes.

5. Remove kebabs from grill, season, and drizzle with balsamic vinegar.

Serves 4.

(Summer Vegetable Kebabs are shown in the photo opposite the next page.)

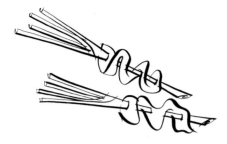

South Seas Chicken Satays

4	**boneless, skinless chicken breast halves**
1 cup	**Malaysian Spice Paste** (*p. 54*) 250 ml
	vegetable oil (*for basting*)
squeeze	**lemon** *or* **lime juice**
	fresh coriander, *chopped* (*optional; for garnish*)

TIPS:

• For a special presentation, thread some of the chicken on slender lemon grass stalks. Soak the stalks for an hour in water and peel off the outer layers if the stalks are fat. You'll also need to pierce the chicken with a skewer before threading it on the lemon grass.

• You can substitute a good-quality ready-prepared Malaysian, Indonesian or Thai spice paste for the homemade one. (See The Asian Cupboard, p. 8.)

• *The wonderful aroma of these satays will draw a crowd to the barbecue to see what's cooking. Serve them for dinner accompanied by warm peanut sauce (p. 24) for dipping and steamed basmati rice, or make smaller satays for appetizers or party snacks.*

1. Pound chicken breasts lightly to flatten; if they are large, slice them in half horizontally and then pound lightly. Cut into strips about 1¼" (3 cm) wide.

2. Coat strips on all sides with Malaysian Spice Paste and refrigerate, covered, several hours or as long as overnight.

3. Soak bamboo skewers in water for about an hour. (You'll need about 12 10"/25 cm skewers for dinner satays, or 24 6"/15 cm skewers for appetizers.)

4. Thread chicken strips on soaked skewers, using 2 strips per skewer for dinner satays and 1 strip per skewer for appetizer satays. Place on a hot, lightly oiled grill over high heat. Grill for 6–8 minutes, turning and basting with a little oil until nicely browned and cooked through.

5. Serve hot, sprinkled with a squeeze of fresh lemon or lime juice and fresh chopped coriander, and warm peanut sauce on the side for dipping.

Serves 4 for dinner or makes about 24 appetizer-sized satays.

Clockwise from front left: South Seas Chicken Satays (this page), Lamb Koftas (p. 55), Summer Vegetable Kebabs (p. 51), and Grilled Mint Julep Peaches (p. 183).

Malaysian Spice Paste

Malaysian Spice Mix

2 tbsp	cumin	30 ml
2 tbsp	coriander	30 ml
2 tbsp	turmeric	30 ml
2 tsp	cinnamon	10 ml
2 tsp	freshly ground black pepper	10 ml
2 tsp	kosher *or* sea salt	10 ml
½ tsp	cayenne *or* ground chili flakes *(optional)*	2 ml

Malaysian Spice Paste

2 tbsp	Malaysian Spice Mix	30 ml
4	green onions, *trimmed*	
1 tbsp	fresh ginger, *chopped*	15 ml
2 strips	lemon zest	
2 tbsp	lemon juice	30 ml
2 tbsp	soy sauce	30 ml
3 tbsp	vegetable oil	45 ml

• *This spice paste starts with a mix of dry spices, which can be made ahead of time. The paste then whirls together in seconds in a blender or food processor (or you can use muscle power and a mortar and pestle) – ready to make South Seas Chicken Satays (p. 52). It's also delicious on pork, fish, or seafood.*

1. Combine ingredients for Malaysian Spice Mix and store in a covered container. *Makes a scant ½ cup (120 ml).*

2. Combine ingredients for Malaysian Spice Paste in a blender or processor and whirl briefly to form a paste. Or finely mince green onions and ginger, chop 2 tsp (10 ml) lemon zest, and pound ingredients together using a mortar and pestle. *Makes about ¾ cup (175 ml).*

TIP:

• The spice paste should be used within a few hours of preparation. The spice mix will stay fresh for a month or two. (The recipe makes enough for several batches of the paste.)

Lamb Koftas

2 lbs	ground lamb	1 kg
1	medium onion, *finely chopped*	
4 cloves	garlic, *minced*	
2 tbsp	fresh dill, *chopped*	30 ml
¼ cup	fresh mint, *chopped*	60 ml
2 tsp	lemon zest, *grated*	10 ml
1½ tsp	salt	7 ml
1 tsp	cumin	5 ml
	freshly ground black pepper	

VARIATION:

• Form the mixture into patties and grill. Tuck the patties into the pockets of warm pita breads and add roasted peppers, crumbled feta cheese, and Mint Yogurt Sauce (p. 67). A great alternative when you're tired of the basic burger!

• *These tasty skewers of ground lamb are sweetly spiced with flavours of the Middle East. Serve with baba ghanouj (a grilled eggplant purée that's available in many supermarkets), finely chopped onion and tomato, Taratoor Sauce (p. 67) or Mint Yogurt Sauce (p. 67), and warm pita breads.*

1. Soak 32 bamboo skewers in water for about an hour.

2. Combine meat, onion, garlic, herbs, lemon zest, and seasonings. Squeeze mixture with your hands, mixing until well blended and smooth.

3. Wet hands lightly, divide mixture into 32 equal portions, and form into uniform cylinder shapes. Thread each cylinder onto a damp bamboo skewer and set on a baking sheet. Cover with plastic wrap and refrigerate several hours or as long as overnight.

4. Remove from the refrigerator 30 minutes before cooking. Place skewers on a hot, lightly oiled grill over high heat. Grill for 8–10 minutes, turning until nicely browned and cooked through.

Serves 4–6.

(Lamb Koftas are shown in the photo opposite p. 52.)

Barbecued Pork Tenderloin
with 3/3/3 Sauce

2	pork tenderloins	
	(about ³/₄ lb/350 g each)	
¹/₃ cup	soy sauce	75 ml
¹/₃ cup	Dijon *or* other prepared mustard	75 ml
¹/₃ cup	honey	75 ml
1 clove	garlic, *minced*	

ALSO GREAT WITH:

• Try this marinade on chicken pieces, too.

• *With only a 15-minute marinating period, this dish is very fast and easy. Wonderful with rice and grilled or stir-fried vegetables.*

1. Trim any visible fat and membrane from the meat.

2. Combine remaining ingredients. Pour over meat, turning the pork to coat thoroughly with marinade. Set aside for about 15 minutes.

3. Preheat barbecue to high and lightly oil the grill. Place meat on the grill; adjust heat to medium-high. Turn meat frequently, brushing lavishly with sauce until done, about 10–12 minutes. (The outside will start to caramelize and the inside should be pink.) Slice and serve immediately.

Serves 4.

Peppered Sirloin Steak

2–3 lbs	**sirloin steak,** *1½" (4 cm) thick*	1–1.5 kg
1 clove	**garlic,** *halved*	
1 tbsp	**olive oil** *or* **cognac**	15 ml
	kosher *or* **sea salt**	
2 tbsp	**black** *or* **mixed peppercorns** *(black, white, green, red), coarsely ground or cracked*	30 ml

TIP:

• The steak can be given its pepper coating up to 24 hours ahead of time. Cover with plastic wrap and refrigerate. Bring the steak to room temperature before you begin the cooking.

A steak grilled to perfection – nicely charred on the outside and tender and juicy within. Ask the butcher to cut a first-class piece of beef for you, and just season simply. (Though a pat of herb butter – see Variation, p. 63 – melting on the grilled steak at serving time would be delicious.) Serve the sirloin with grilled vegetables and a baked potato, or sun-ripened field tomatoes and corn on the cob.

1. Rub the steak with the cut clove of garlic and the oil or cognac, and salt lightly. Pat an even coating of black pepper on both sides of the meat.

2. Preheat the barbecue and lightly oil the grill rack. Grill the steak about 8 minutes per side over medium-high heat for medium-rare. Remove the steak from the grill when it is just a bit more rare than you like it.

3. Allow to rest for 5 minutes. Serve in slices cut across the grain with all the trimmings.

Serves 4–6.

Dilly Potato Skewers

16	mini new potatoes, *of uniform size*	
2 tbsp	olive oil	30 ml
2 tbsp	butter, *melted*	30 ml
	kosher *or* sea salt	
¼ cup	fresh dill, *chopped*	60 ml
2 tbsp	chives *or* green onions, *finely chopped*	30 ml

TIP:

•It's easier to control grilling time if you don't combine vegetables on the same skewer with fish or meat. Cook vegetables on skewers first and set them to the side of the grill, then quickly grill the meat or fish, which is best enjoyed piping hot straight from the fire. (If you do include vegetables with meat or fish on the same skewer, choose varieties that require the same degree of heat and the same cooking time.)

• *These crispy little potatoes are a good accompaniment to almost any simply grilled fish or meat.*

1. Lightly oil 4 metal skewers.

2. Toss potatoes with olive oil and thread on skewers.

3. Place on a clean, hot, lightly oiled grill over medium heat, or at the edge of the fire. Turn regularly until potatoes are tender – 20–40 minutes, depending on size.

4. Towards the end of the cooking time, move skewers to a hot area of the grill to crisp the skin.

5. Gently push potatoes from the skewers into a warm bowl and toss with melted butter, salt, and herbs.

Serves 4.

TIPS:

• Use metal skewers to grill potatoes, as they transfer heat effectively and speed up the cooking.

• An easy alternate method: Grill the potatoes in a vegetable grilling basket. Toss them a few times during cooking so they crisp evenly.

Pork Satays with Orange Ginger Glaze

1½ lbs	pork tenderloin	750 g

Orange Ginger Marinade

1	small onion, *finely chopped*	
1 tbsp	ginger, *finely minced*	15 ml
1 tsp	garlic, *finely chopped*	5 ml
4 strips	orange zest, *cut in slivers*	
½ cup	Chinese rice wine or **dry sherry**	125 ml
¼ cup	soy sauce	60 ml
¼ cup	maple syrup	60 ml
1 tbsp	sesame oil	15 ml

VARIATIONS:

• Orange Ginger Glazed Sweet Potatoes: Peel potatoes and cut ino 1" (2.5 cm) cubes. Thread on metal skewers and grill over medium heat. Turn and baste with marinade until tender, about 15–20 minutes. Brush with glaze as above (Step 4) and sprinkle with toasted sesame seeds.

• The Orange Ginger Marinade is also great on chicken and fish.

• *Strips of skewered tender pork with a light citrus glaze make a mouth-watering meal accompanied by fragrant basmati rice or Orange Ginger Glazed Sweet Potatoes (Variation, below) and a crunchy salad of snow and snap peas. Alternatively, make smaller skewers and serve as appetizers or party snacks.*

1. Trim meat. Cut the tenderloin in half crosswise. Then slice each piece through the middle so you have 4 thin pieces. Pound to flatten. Cut each piece into strips about ¾"–1" (2–2.5 cm) wide.

2. Combine all ingredients for Orange Ginger Marinade. Coat pork strips with marinade, cover, and leave for several hours in the refrigerator.

3. Soak bamboo skewers in water for an hour or so – short ones for appetizer satays, 10" (2.5 cm) ones for dinner satays.

4. When ready to cook, remove pork from marinade and pat dry. Reserve about a third of the marinade for basting. Strain the remainder into a small saucepan, bring to a boil, and boil for about 5 minutes, reducing to form a syrupy glaze.

5. Thread 2 pork strips on each skewer for dinner satays, one per skewer for appetizers, and place on a hot, lightly oiled grill over high heat. Grill for 6–8 minutes, turning several times and basting with marinade until nicely browned and cooked through. Remove from grill and brush with glaze.

Serves 4 for dinner. Makes about 16 appetizer-sized satays.

Cedar-Smoked Salmon & Trout

1	**untreated cedar plank,** *approx. ¾" x 8" x 16"*	
1	**skin-on salmon fillet,** *about 2–2½ lbs (1 kg)* **or**	
2–2½ lbs	**trout fillets**	1 kg
3 tbsp	**olive oil**	45 ml
1	**small onion,** *finely chopped*	
2 cloves	**garlic,** *minced*	
2 tbsp	**peppercorns,** *coarsely ground*	30 ml
4 tbsp	**fresh dill,** *finely chopped*	60 ml

TIP:

• Check a few times to make sure the plank is not catching fire. Douse flare-ups with water from a spray bottle. If necessary, elevate the plank on small "logs" of crumpled-up aluminum foil to get it farther from the fire.

• *Plank cooking is a technique of Native origins that imparts a subtle smoky flavour to fish. It's also a fabulous, easy way to cook fish for a crowd. (You can achieve the same effect, though, by using small cedar sticks placed directly on the fire; see tips, p. 9.) Be prepared for the amount of smoke you create!*

1. Soak the untreated cedar plank in water for at least an hour. Drain and rub one side with a little olive oil.

2. Brush the fish with olive oil and sprinkle with salt. Combine onion, garlic, peppercorns, and dill, and pat the mixture onto the flesh side of the fish to form a crust.

3. Preheat the barbecue. Place the fish skin side down on the side of the cedar plank that was rubbed with oil, tent it with aluminum foil, and place it on the grill over medium-high heat. (If you're using small cedar sticks instead of a plank, place the fish on heavy-duty aluminum foil that has been brushed with olive oil.)

4. Cook with the cover down for about 20–30 minutes for 1 large fillet, 10 minutes for smaller ones, or until fish is just opaque at the thickest part. (Time will vary with size of fillet.) Remove plank and fish from grill, and brush fish with a little more olive oil. Transfer fish to a platter and serve immediately, garnished with lemon slices and chopped fresh dill.

Serves 6–8.

Cedar-smoked fish is moist and flavourful. (Don't overcook it!) Just be sure to use cedar that hasn't been treated.

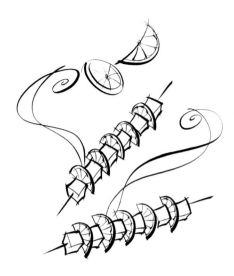

¾ lb	**salmon**	**375 g**
¾ lb	**grouper, sea bass, tuna,** *or* **other firm-fleshed fish**	**375 g**
2	**lemons**	
4	**green onions,** *trimmed*	
½ cup	**Spicy Lemon Garlic Butter** *(facing page), melted*	**125 ml**

TIP:

• If you're alternating different elements or colours on skewers, as with this recipe, lay them out in order on your cutting board first. This "dry run" helps ensure you get the right number of pieces in the right sequence on each skewer, and makes the job of threading them on the sticks faster.

Skewered Fish
with Spicy Lemon Garlic Butter

• *Firm-fleshed fish is well suited to grilling. The only trick is to be sure not to overcook it – take it off the barbecue as soon as it turns opaque. Serve the kebabs with Dilly Potato Skewers (p. 58) and Grilled Asparagus (p. 50).*

1. Soak 4 10" (25 cm) bamboo skewers in water for about an hour.

2. Trim the fish, removing any skin and stray bones, and cut each fish into 12 equal pieces.

3. Slice the lemons thinly crosswise, and cut each slice in half. Cut each green onion into 3 pieces.

4. Thread fish (6 pieces per skewer), lemon, and green onion pieces alternately onto the skewers, sandwiching the lemon slices tightly between the pieces of fish.

5. Brush the skewers with a light coating of the melted spicy butter and set on a clean, lightly oiled grill over medium heat. After about 4 minutes, turn and baste lightly.

6. Continue grilling until the fish is opaque and just cooked, about 3–4 minutes more. Serve hot with fresh lemon slices on the side and the remaining melted butter for those who would like it.

Serves 4.

Spicy Lemon Garlic Butter

½ lb	**unsalted butter,** *softened*	**250 g**
4	**green onions,** *finely chopped*	
3 cloves	**garlic,** *minced*	
2 tsp	**lemon zest,** *grated*	**10 ml**
1 tbsp	**fresh thyme,** *chopped* **or**	**15 ml**
1 tsp	**dried thyme**	**5 ml**
1 tbsp	**Worcestershire sauce**	**15 ml**
good pinch	**cayenne** **or**	
dash	**hot sauce**	
½ tsp	**salt**	**2 ml**
½ tsp	**freshly ground black pepper**	**2 ml**

• *Use this spicy butter as a baste for seafood and lamb, or to top a baked potato.*

1. Thoroughly combine all ingredients using a food processor, a mortar and pestle, or a fork and a shallow bowl. Spoon the flavoured butter onto a sheet of wax paper or foil and form into a log.

2. Wrap securely and refrigerate or freeze.

Makes about 1 cup (250 ml).

TIPS:

• You can make the flavoured butter ahead and store it for a couple of days in the refrigerator or for a month or so in the freezer.

• For a party snack or appetizer, use the Spicy Lemon Garlic Butter to baste skewers with a large shrimp curled around a sea scallop on each. Grill for about 2–3 minutes per side, turning and basting, until the seafood is opaque.

VARIATION:

• Tarragon Butter: Use the same technique, except mix the butter with 2 tbsp (30 ml) chopped fresh tarragon (or 2 tsp/10 ml dried), 2 tsp (10 ml) grated lemon zest, 2 tbsp (30 ml) fresh lemon juice, and kosher or sea salt to taste. Slice off pats as needed. Great on top of grilled steak, grilled fish, or a baked potato.

Cumin-Scented Leg of Lamb

2–3 lbs	boneless leg of lamb	1–1.5 kg
1 tsp	ground cumin	5 ml
½ tsp	cayenne	2 ml
1 tsp	coarsely ground black pepper	5 ml
1 tsp	kosher *or* sea salt	5 ml
4 cloves	garlic, *minced*	
1 tbsp	olive oil	15 ml
	Cumin Salt (*see Quick Trick, below*)	

TIPS:

• This spice paste is also great on lamb kebabs. Cut the meat into cubes, toss them with the paste, and thread on skewers. Grill 8–10 minutes, until the meat is nicely browned outside and tender and juicy within.

•The lemony flavour of cumin comes through best if you lightly toast whole cumin seeds in a heavy skillet for 2–3 minutes over medium heat, just until the aroma is released, then grind them in a spice mill.

• *Serve this boned leg of lamb with its spicy crust cut in thin slices across the grain, with a sprinkle of Cumin Salt on top and a dollop of Mint Yogurt Sauce (p. 67) on the side. Rice pilaf or lemon rosemary roasted potatoes, and Cumin Carrot Salad (p. 82) or a sliced tomato salad with crumbled feta, black olives, and a light vinaigrette are good accompaniments.*

1. Spread out boned leg of lamb, trim away excess fat or sinew, and pound lightly to flatten. Slash the thickest parts to make the piece lie flat.

2. Combine remaining ingredients in a small bowl to make a paste, and rub into the lamb on all sides. Place, covered, in a shallow pan or heavy-duty plastic bag and leave to marinate in the refrigerator several hours or overnight.

3. Remove lamb from refrigerator an hour before cooking. Place on a pre-heated grill over medium-high indirect heat (see p. 9), with a drip pan underneath. Roast 30–40 minutes, turning once, for medium rare. Remove the meat when the internal temperature is just below 140°F (60°C) for rare; 150°F (70°C) for medium. Let rest for 10 minutes before slicing.

Serves 6–8.

QUICK TRICK:

A pinch or two of Cumin Salt really brings out the flavour of grilled lamb. Just combine equal amounts of freshly toasted ground cumin seed and sea salt and sprinkle on the meat before serving.

Grilled Cumin-Scented Leg of Lamb served with Mint Yogurt Sauce (p. 67), Cumin Carrot Salad (p. 82), and Potato Salad with Asparagus (p. 75).

Maple-Glazed and Thai Green Curry
Chicken Wings

24	chicken wings	

Maple Marinade & Basting Sauce

½ cup	maple syrup	125 ml
2 tbsp	brown sugar	30 ml
¼ cup	ketchup	60 ml
1 tbsp	apple cider vinegar	15 ml
1 tbsp	Worcestershire sauce	15 ml
1 tbsp	lemon juice	15 ml
1 tsp	dry mustard	5 ml
1 clove	garlic, *finely chopped*	
dash	Tabasco *or* hot sauce	
	salt and freshly ground black pepper	

Thai Green Curry Marinade & Sauce

¼–½ cup	green curry paste	60–125 ml
1 can	coconut milk	400 ml
½ tsp	salt	2 ml

• *The maple-glazed wings are popular with kids, the aromatic glaze providing a hint of sweetness and not too much heat. The Thai Green Curry ones are hotter, but extremely flavourful – and easy, since they start with a prepared paste.*

1. Combine all ingredients for Maple Marinade in a small saucepan. Bring to a boil over moderate heat, stirring to dissolve sugar. Combine all ingredients for Thai Green Curry Marinade in a small bowl.

2. Cut off and discard tips of wings and divide wings at the joint. In a large dish, cover wings with marinade of choice and refrigerate for about 2 hours.

3. Preheat barbecue and lightly oil grill. Remove wings from marinade and cook over medium heat for 10 minutes. Turn wings, baste with marinade, and cook 10 minutes more. Turn, baste, and continue to cook until wings are crisp, about 10–15 minutes longer.

Makes 48 pieces.

ALSO GREAT WITH:

• The Maple Marinade & Basting Sauce is also delicious on ribs, sausages, and other chicken pieces, so make a double batch. (It will keep in the refrigerator for several weeks.) You'll need to parboil or precook ribs and sausages before glazing with the sauce. The Thai Green Curry Marinade is delicious on any type of chicken pieces.

TIP:

• Wings can also be cooked in the oven. Spread in a single layer on a baking sheet and bake at 400˚F (200˚C). Turn and baste occasionally until wings are nicely browned on the outside and tender and cooked inside, about 30 minutes.

Great Sauces for Grilled Food

Taratoor Sauce

½ cup	tahini	125 ml
2 cloves	garlic, *finely minced*	
⅓ cup	fresh lemon juice	75 ml
4–5 tbsp	warm water	60–75 ml
	salt and freshly ground pepper	

Mint Yogurt Sauce

1 cup	plain yogurt	250 ml
½ cup	sour cream	125 ml
1 tbsp	fresh lemon juice	15 ml
2 tbsp	fresh mint, *chopped*	30 ml
¼ tsp	kosher *or* sea salt	1 ml

Mustard Dill Sauce

¼ cup	grainy mustard	60 ml
1 tsp	dry mustard	5 ml
3 tbsp	sugar *or* honey	45 ml
2 tbsp	white wine vinegar	30 ml
⅓ cup	vegetable oil	75 ml
3 tbsp	fresh dill, *chopped*	45 ml

Taratoor Sauce

This Middle Eastern sauce is a traditional accompaniment to Lamb Koftas (p. 55), but it's also delicious with other grilled lamb dishes, beef, and vegetables.

1. Combine ingredients, adding enough warm water to make a sauce of thick pouring consistency. *Makes about ¾ cup (175 ml).*

Mint Yogurt Sauce

Similar to tzatziki, this sauce is also great with grilled lamb or vegetables. Try it with Cumin-Scented Leg of Lamb (p. 65) or as a dip for grilled asparagus (p. 50).

1. Stir all ingredients together and refrigerate. Taste and adjust seasoning before serving. *Makes 1½ cups (375 ml).*

Grainy Mustard Dill Sauce

Baste pork or chicken with this sauce, then serve it alongside the grilled meat. Mix it with mayo to make a delicious spread for a chicken or ham sandwich.

1. Combine ingredients thoroughly. Adjust sweetness or sharpness to your taste by adding more sugar or vinegar. *Makes about 1 cup (250 ml).*

Pickled Beets with a Bite (p. 92)

CONTENTS

QUICK TRICKS

* These recipes are main-dish salads, or include a variation for a main-dish salad

MAIN DISH SALAD

CROWD PLEASERS

Elegant, Expandable Feast

The recipes serve 6, but they are easily multiplied for a larger group.

Red Pepper & Feta Spread (*p. 32*) **with Spicy Pita Wedges** (*p. 35*) **and assorted olives**

Cumin-Scented Leg of Lamb (*p. 65*) **with Mint Yogurt Sauce** (*p. 67*)

**Sliced tomato salad with crumbled feta and black olives
or Cumin Carrot Salad** (*p. 82*)

**Lemon rosemary roasted potatoes
or Chickpeas & Roasted Peppers** (*p. 81*)

Ginger Shortbread (*p. 161*) **with Strawberry Rhubarb Compote** (*p. 162*)

A Midsummer Night's Dream (for 6)

Polenta Circles (*p. 28*) **with Roasted Tomato Corn Salsa** (*p. 20*)

Cedar-Smoked Salmon or Trout (*p. 60*)

Potato Salad with Asparagus (*p. 75*)

Simple Tomato Salad (*p. 82*) **or Pickled Beets with a Bite** (*p. 92*)

Warm Breads

Sweet & Simple Peach Tart (*p. 179*)

Casual Mediterranean Meal (for 6)

Grilled Herbed Focaccia (*p. 123*) **with Cottage Tapenade** (*p. 16*) **and/or Simple Tomato Salad Topping** (*p. 82*)

Lazy Summer Paella (*p. 41*)

(Chicken skewers for the kids)

Tossed green salad

Warm crusty bread

Orange-Glazed Pound Cake (*p. 175*), **Lynda's No-Bake Bars** (*p. 157*), **and fresh strawberries**

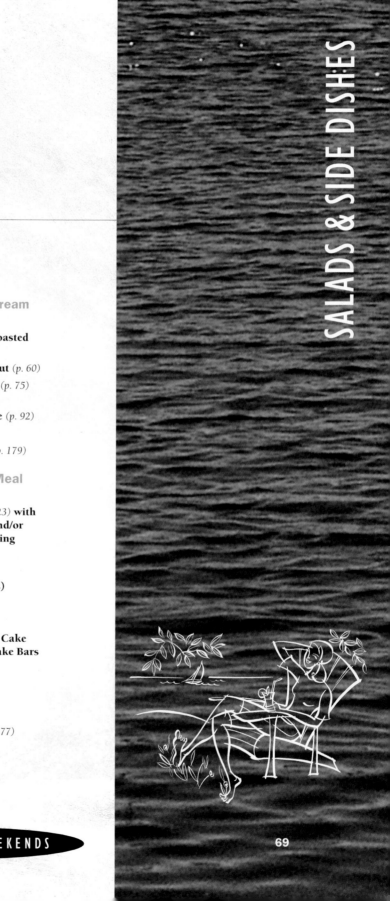

Green Beans & Feta (p. 77)

Classic Dressing

1 clove	garlic, *minced*	
1 tsp	salt	5 ml
1 tbsp	Dijon mustard	15 ml
1/3 cup	vinegar (see Tips, below)	75 ml
1 cup	oil (see Tips, below)	250 ml
	freshly ground black pepper	

TIPS:

• Try red wine, champagne, sherry, balsamic, or rice vinegar, or equal parts fresh lemon juice and vinegar. Olive, corn, and safflower oil are all good choices.

• If you find your dressing is too acidic for your taste, soften the flavour with a scant teaspoonful of honey or sugar.

• *With the addition of different fresh herbs or a little crumbled cheese at serving time, this basic vinaigrette can be used to dress a variety of salads. (Just for starters: It's used in the recipes on pp. 72, 74, 75, and 78.) Mix up a batch and store it in a covered jar in the refrigerator – it will keep for up to 10 days. Use 3–4 tbsp (45–60 ml) of dressing for every 4–5 cups (1–1.2 L) of greens.*

1. Mash garlic with salt, then mix with mustard and vinegar.

2. Whisk in oil and season to taste.

Makes 1 1/3 cups (325 ml).

QUICK TRICK:

A handful of crispy croutons adds extra crunch to green salads: Cut homemade-style bread into cubes to make about 6 cups (1.5 L). Toss with salt and pepper, 3 tbsp (45 ml) olive oil – or part oil, part melted butter – and other seasonings if desired: 2 tsp (10 ml) dried herbs, a clove of minced garlic, a dash of hot sauce or chili flakes, and/or 2 tbsp (30 ml) Parmesan cheese. Spread croutons on a baking sheet and bake at 375°F (190°C) for 10–15 minutes until crisp and golden, shaking a few times during baking. Cool and store in a covered container.

A Quartet of Green Salads

TIPS:

• To prepare greens ahead, wrap the washed and dried leaves loosely in paper towel or a tea towel and store in a perforated plastic bag in the vegetable crisper.

• Soft-textured, mild-flavoured salad greens, such as bibb lettuce and Boston lettuce, spoil quickly and do not travel or keep well. Crisper varieties, such as romaine and leaf and red leaf lettuce, are hardier. So are greens such as endive, escarole, frisée, dandelion, young spinach, arugula, watercress, and radicchio.

• Hydroponically grown greens, with their roots still attached, are sold in some supermarkets. This lengthens their refrigerator life and allows them to travel better.

• *Each of these salads uses a variation of the Classic Dressing (facing page). You'll need about 4–5 cups (1–1.2 L) of greens for each, which will serve 4 people.*

Arugula Orange Salad

To a scant ¹/₄ cup (60 ml) Classic Dressing, add 1 tsp (5 ml) walnut oil and 1 tbsp (15 ml) orange juice. Mix with 1 tsp (5 ml) grated orange rind, and toss with young arugula. Add peeled orange segments and toasted walnuts.

Spinach Mushroom Salad

To a scant ¹/₄ cup (60 ml) Classic Dressing, add 1 tbsp (15 ml) fresh lemon juice, 1 tsp (5 ml) grated lemon rind, and 1 tsp (5 ml) fresh chopped tarragon or ¹/₂ tsp (2 ml) dried tarragon. Toss with spinach leaves. Add sliced fresh mushrooms, thinly sliced red onion rings, and crumbled crispy bacon.

Romaine Blue Cheese Salad

To ¹/₄ cup (60 ml) Classic Dressing, add 2 oz (60 g) mashed blue cheese. Toss with romaine leaves, thinly sliced red onion rings, and a handful of croutons. Top with more crumbled blue cheese, if you like.

Cheater's Caesar Salad

To ¹/₄ cup (60 ml) Classic Dressing made with half lemon juice, half vinegar, add 1 anchovy fillet and 2 tbsp (30 ml) grated Parmesan cheese. Mash anchovy into dressing. Toss with romaine leaves, add a handful of croutons, and sprinkle with more grated Parmesan.

Wheat Berry Salad
with Wild Rice & Orzo

1½ cups	wheat berries	325 ml
½ cup	wild rice	125 ml
1 cup	orzo	250 ml
½	medium red onion, *finely chopped*	
2	green onions, *finely chopped*	
2 stalks	celery, *finely chopped*	
1	zucchini, *grated*	
½ cup	fresh parsley, *finely chopped*	125 ml
	arugula *or* romaine lettuce leaves	
½ cup	Classic Dressing *(p. 70), made with olive oil and red wine vinegar*	125 ml

• *Wheat berries (whole, unprocessed kernels of wheat) and orzo (a rice-shaped pasta) have been "discovered" by North American cooks recently. They are easy to prepare and add lots of flavour, goodness, and satisfying texture to salads.*

1. Bring a large pot of lightly salted water to a boil. Add the wheat berries and cook for 10 minutes. Add the wild rice to the same pot and continue cooking for 30 minutes more, or until grains are tender. In another pot, cook the orzo in lightly salted water for 10–15 minutes. Drain grains and orzo well.

2. In a large bowl combine cooked grains and pasta with onions, celery, zucchini, and parsley and toss with vinaigrette, reserving a couple of tablespoons of dressing.

3. At serving time, either pile the salad on a platter lined with arugula or romaine, or tear up some of the green leaves and toss with the salad. Taste and adjust seasoning, adding a little more dressing if needed.

Serves 8–10.

TIPS:

• Look for wheat berries – also called "hard wheat kernels" – in bulk-food and natural-food stores. You'll find orzo in boxes in the pasta section of the supermarket, as well as in bulk-food stores.

• The salad can be made ahead (through Step 2) and will keep in the refrigerator for a couple of days.

Both Wheat Berry Salad with Wild Rice & Orzo and Tuscan Pepper & Tomato Salad (p. 74) are real standouts on a potluck or party table.

Tuscan Pepper & Tomato Salad

2	red peppers	
1	yellow pepper	
1	green pepper	
1	jalapeño pepper *(optional)*	
1	medium red onion, *thinly sliced*	
1 pint	cherry tomatoes, *halved*	500 ml
¼ cup	black olives, *pitted*	60 ml
¼ cup	Classic Dressing *(p. 70), made with red wine or balsamic vinegar and extra-virgin olive oil*	60 ml
¼ tsp	chili flakes	1 ml
1 tbsp	fresh basil *or* part basil, part oregano, *chopped*	15 ml
	fresh greens *(such as arugula, romaine, and endive)*	
	salt and freshly ground black pepper	

• *Every bite of this crisp salad says summer. Very colourful, it looks fabulous on the table. Serve it alongside Pepper-Encrusted Loin of Pork (p. 44), Lemon Rosemary Turkey or Chicken (p. 42), or Skewered Fish (p. 62).*

1. Halve all peppers lengthwise. Remove seeds and core, and cut into very fine slices.

2. In a large bowl toss the peppers, onion, tomatoes, and olives with the dressing, chili flakes, and herbs. Adjust seasoning.

3. Line a platter with a bed of crisp greens and arrange the salad on top.

Serves 4.

TIP:

• The peppers and onion can be prepared a few hours ahead, but add the tomatoes just before serving, as they tend to become soft and release their juices.

MAIN-DISH VARIATION:

• Add slices of bocconcini (or regular mozzarella) and salami, or chunks of grilled tuna to the platter.

(Tuscan Pepper & Tomato Salad is shown in the photo on the previous page.)

Potato Salad with Asparagus

2 lbs	**small new potatoes**	1 kg
½ cup	**dry white wine**	125 ml
1 lb	**asparagus**	500 g
4 oz	**snow peas**	125 g
½	**medium red onion,** *finely chopped*	
4	**green onions,** *finely chopped*	
¼ cup	**fresh dill,** *chopped*	60 ml
½ cup	**Classic Dressing** *(p.70), made with white wine or balsamic vinegar and a fruity extra-virgin olive oil*	125 ml
	salt and freshly ground black pepper	

MAIN-DISH VARIATION:

• Garnish the salad with slivered prosciutto or shaved smoked ham and hard-cooked eggs, quartered length-wise. Or top with skewers of tender grilled shrimp (p. 41).

• *Potato salad becomes a standout dish with the addition of blanched vegetables such as asparagus and snow peas.*

1. Cover potatoes with salted water and boil until just tender. (Test them after 10 minutes; they will continue to cook for a few minutes after they are drained.) Drain, remove skins if desired, and halve or quarter.

2. Sprinkle the warm potatoes with wine and salt and pepper, then toss so the liquid will be evenly absorbed.

3. Trim asparagus and snow peas. Blanch asparagus in boiling, lightly salted water until just tender, about 3–5 minutes, depending on the thickness of the stem. In another pot, blanch the snow peas for a minute or so. Drain well. Wrap and chill until needed.

4. Add chopped onions, dill, and almost all of the dressing to the potatoes.

5. At serving time, slice the asparagus and snow peas on the diagonal into bite-sized pieces. Toss with a little dressing and arrange over the potatoes, or toss all together. Season to taste and sprinkle with additional fresh dill.

Serves 6.

TIP:

•You can prepare the elements of the salad a few hours ahead and combine them at serving time.

(Potato Salad with Asparagus is shown in the photo opposite p. 65.)

Green Beans & Feta
with Sun-Dried Tomato Vinaigrette

¾ lb	**green beans,** *trimmed*	375 g
	leaf lettuce leaves	
½ lb	**feta cheese,** *cut in cubes*	250 g
4	**sun-dried tomatoes,** *packed in oil*	
⅓ cup	**kalamata olives**	75 ml
1–2 tbsp	**chives** *or* **green onions,** *chopped*	15–30 ml

Sun-Dried Tomato Vinaigrette

2	**sun-dried tomatoes,** *packed in oil*	
3 tbsp	**red wine vinegar**	45 ml
1 clove	**garlic,** *minced*	
1 tbsp	**fresh oregano,** *minced* **or**	15 ml
1 tsp	**dried oregano**	5 ml
1 tsp	**sugar**	5 ml
	salt and freshly ground black pepper	
⅓ cup	**olive oil**	75 ml

This Mediterranean-inspired salad makes a good accompaniment to grilled meats. Or it can be served on individual plates as a salad course.

1. To make the vinaigrette, finely chop the 2 sun-dried tomatoes and whisk together with the vinegar, garlic, oregano, sugar, salt, and pepper until blended. Slowly drizzle in oil, whisking constantly until emulsified.

2. Steam beans until tender-crisp. Plunge into cold water to stop the cooking, then drain and wrap in paper towel. Chill until ready to serve.

3. Line a platter with lettuce leaves. Arrange half the beans on top of the lettuce. Top with feta cubes, then put remaining beans over cheese. Slice remaining 4 tomatoes into thin strips and scatter with olives around beans.

4. Drizzle vinaigrette over salad. Sprinkle with chives or green onions and garnish with additional oregano leaves, if you wish.

Serves 4.

TIPS:
• Dressing can be made ahead and stored, covered, in the refrigerator for up to 1 week.

• If oil-packed tomatoes are not available, dried tomatoes that have been rehydrated work equally well.

MAIN-DISH VARIATION:
• Top the salad with chunks of grilled tuna, and serve with crusty bread.

Feta cheese, olives, and sun-dried tomatoes give the green beans zip. This salad goes together quickly and expands easily.

Roasted Vegetable Pasta Salad

1	**medium eggplant,** *sliced*	
2	**zucchini,** *sliced lengthwise*	
1	**red onion,** *cut in eighths*	
2	**sweet peppers,** *sliced lengthwise in quarters*	
2 cloves	**garlic,** *sliced*	
2 tbsp	**olive oil**	**30 ml**
½ lb	**fusilli** *or* **farfalle pasta**	**250 g**
½ cup	**Classic Dressing** *(p. 70), made with red wine or balsamic vinegar and olive oil*	**125 ml**
¼ cup	**fresh basil,** *chopped*	**60 ml**
4 oz	**goat cheese,** *crumbled (optional)*	**125 g**
	salt and freshly ground black pepper	

MAIN-DISH VARIATION:

• Arrange salad on a platter and top with thin slices of cold grilled sirloin steak. Omit the goat cheese and garnish with shavings of Parmesan and a handful of black olives.

• *A great salad for taking to a picnic or potluck, since it can be made entirely ahead. Grill the vegetables when you've got the barbecue on for another meal.*

1. Toss vegetables with garlic, oil, and salt and pepper.

2. Arrange vegetables on lightly oiled, preheated barbecue grill and cook over medium-high heat approximately 5–10 minutes on each side until tender and lightly browned.

3. Cook pasta in a large pot of boiling, salted water until just tender; test after 8 minutes. Drain, refresh under cold water, and drain thoroughly again. Turn into a large bowl and toss with a little dressing.

4. Cut grilled vegetables into rough chunks and toss with pasta, dressing, basil, and goat cheese. Season to taste and refrigerate. Bring to room temperature before serving.

Serves 4–6.

TIPS:

• Pan-roast the vegetables if you prefer: Toss them with oil, garlic and seasonings as above, and spread in a single layer in a large, shallow roasting pan. Roast in a 400°F (200°C) oven about 30 minutes, until vegetables are tender and nicely browned, turning halfway through.

• You can use any combination of grilled or pan-roasted vegetables in this salad, making sure you have a total of about 3–4 cups (750 ml–1 L).

Roasted Vegetable Gratin

1 can	Italian-style plum tomatoes *(28 oz/790 ml)*	
6 cups	pan-roasted *or* grilled vegetables *(eggplant, zucchini, yellow zucchini, onion, red pepper, garlic), cut into chunks*	1.5 L
1 cup	dry bread crumbs *or* crushed croutons	250 ml
½ cup	fresh parsley, *chopped*	125 ml
1 cup	mozzarella cheese, *coarsely grated*	250 ml
2 tbsp	Parmesan cheese, *grated*	30 ml
1 tbsp	olive oil	15 ml
	salt and freshly ground black pepper	

• *A gratin is essentially a baked casserole with a crisp crust. Served with warm bread and a green salad (pp. 70–71), this gratin makes an excellent meatless dinner. It's also a good way to use leftover grilled or roasted vegetables. (For instructions on pan-roasting and grilling vegetables, see the facing page.)*

1. Drain and chop tomatoes, reserving juice. Toss tomatoes with vegetables, adding enough juice so mixture is moist. Season and spread into a shallow casserole.

2. Combine breadcrumbs, parsley, and cheeses. Spread in an even layer on top of the vegetable mixture. Drizzle oil on top.

3. Bake at 400°F (200°C) for about 15 minutes until vegetables are bubbling and cheese is melted. Serve hot or at room temperature.

Serves 4.

TIP:
• As an alternative, place half the vegetables in the casserole and sprinkle with half the bread-crumb mixture. Spoon in remaining vegetables and top with remaining bread crumbs. Bake as above.

VARIATION:
• You can make the roasted vegetable salad on the facing page with couscous instead of pasta. Cover 1 cup (250 ml) couscous with 1 cup (250 ml) hot stock and leave for 5 minutes. Fluff the grains with a fork, adding a splash of lemon juice and olive oil, and proceed with the recipe.

White Bean & Spinach Salad

6 tbsp	**extra-virgin olive oil**	90 ml
½	**medium red onion,** *thinly sliced*	
1 clove	**garlic,** *finely chopped*	
1 tsp	**ground coriander**	5 ml
1 bunch	**young spinach,** *trimmed, washed, and dried*	
2 tbsp	**lemon juice**	30 ml
1 can	**white beans,** *rinsed and drained (19 oz/540 ml)*	
3–4 oz	**feta cheese,** *crumbled (optional)*	100–125 g
	salt and freshly ground black pepper	

MAIN-DISH VARIATION:

• Garnish salad with grilled sliced lamb or lamb kebabs, or slices of grilled sausages.

• *This simple salad takes only minutes to prepare. It can be served at room temperature or chilled.*

1. Heat 2 tbsp (30 ml) of the olive oil in a large frying pan over moderate heat. Add onion and garlic and cook until soft. Stir in coriander.

2. Add spinach, sprinkle with a little salt, and cover pan. Let spinach steam until just wilted. Set aside.

3. Mix lemon juice with remaining olive oil. Season with salt and pepper to taste.

4. Combine spinach-onion mixture with beans and toss with lemon dressing. Adjust seasoning. Sprinkle crumbled feta cheese on top.

Serves 4.

TIPS:

• If fresh spinach isn't available, use a package of frozen leaf spinach, thawed and thoroughly patted dry.

• The salad can be made a few hours before serving.

Chickpeas & Roasted Peppers

1 can	**chickpeas,** *rinsed and drained (19 oz/540 ml)*	
2	**red peppers,** *roasted, peeled, seeded, and sliced*	
1	**yellow pepper,** *roasted, peeled, seeded, and sliced*	
½	**small red onion,** *finely chopped*	
¼ cup	**fresh parsley,** *chopped*	60 ml
2 stalks	**celery,** *cut into fine matchstick lengths*	
1	**carrot,** *cut into fine matchstick lengths*	

Dressing

1–2 cloves	**garlic,** *minced*	
½ tsp	**dried oregano**	2 ml
3 tbsp	**red wine vinegar**	45 ml
½ cup	**olive oil**	125 ml
	salt and freshly ground black pepper	

- *A colourful salad that travels and keeps well.*

1. To make the dressing, mash garlic with a little salt and whisk in the remaining ingredients.

2. Combine chickpeas with peppers, onion, and parsley. Toss with the dressing, reserving about 3 tbsp (45 ml). Mound the chickpea mixture on a shallow platter.

3. Toss celery and carrot sticks in the remaining dressing. Arrange on the platter around the chickpeas, or simply combine the two mixtures. Serve the salad at room temperature.

Serves 4.

TIP:

• The salad can be made a day ahead and kept, covered, in the refrigerator. Bring to room temperature before serving.

MAIN-DISH VARIATION:

• Add crumbled feta cheese, a handful of black olives, quartered hard-boiled eggs, and slices of Peppered Sirloin (p. 57) or other grilled steak.

Cumin Carrot Salad

2 lbs	sweet young carrots	1 kg
2 cloves	garlic, *unpeeled*	
1	shallot, *finely minced* or	
2	green onions, *finely minced*	
1 tsp	paprika	5 ml
1 tsp	cumin	5 ml
½ tsp	dried hot chili flakes *(optional)*	2 ml
1 tbsp	lemon juice or **rice vinegar**	15 ml
3 tbsp	extra-virgin olive oil	45 ml
¼ tsp	kosher *or* sea salt	1 ml
	freshly ground black pepper	
½ cup	fresh Italian (flat-leaf) parsley, *chopped*	125 ml

• *The delicate taste of this side dish complements a main course with Indian, Moroccan, or Eastern Mediterranean flavours.*

1. Peel carrots, quarter them lengthwise, then cut in half crosswise to make julienne matchsticks of equal size for even cooking.

2. Place carrots in a large saucepan, cover with water, and add garlic cloves. Bring to a boil, cover, lower heat to medium, and cook until carrot sticks are barely tender. Test after 3 minutes. Drain, plunge into ice water to cool quickly, and drain again. Discard garlic.

3. In a small bowl whisk together remaining ingredients except parsley, and toss with carrots.

4. Store, covered, in the refrigerator for up to 24 hours. Serve at room temperature with a topping of fresh chopped parsley.

Serves 6.

QUICK TRICK:

When tomatoes are at their peak, this simple salad is fantastic: Cut 2 large ripe tomatoes in half, then cut each half in narrow wedges. Discard the seeds. Toss the tomato wedges with 2 cloves of slivered garlic, ¼ cup (60 ml) of chopped fresh Italian (flat-leaf) parsley, 1 tbsp (15 ml) each of extra-virgin olive oil and red wine vinegar and salt and freshly ground black pepper. Let the salad sit at room temperature for a half-hour for flavours to blend.

If you chop the tomato wedges into smaller pieces, the salad becomes a topping for slices of grilled garlic bread (bruschetta) or circles of grilled polenta (p. 28).

(Cumin Carrot Salad is shown in the photo opposite p. 65.)

Red Cabbage Salad

1	small red cabbage	
2	medium carrots	
3	green onions, *sliced*	
½ cup	raisins	125 ml
½ cup	walnuts *or* pecans, *chopped and toasted*	125 ml
¼ cup	fresh parsley, *chopped*	60 ml

Lemon Cumin Dressing

2 tbsp	lemon juice	30 ml
2 tsp	brown sugar	10 ml
1 tsp	cumin	5 ml
6 tbsp	olive oil	90 ml
	salt and freshly ground black pepper	

• *Cabbage salads generally stand up well, and this crisp, colourful one is no exception. It travels happily to a potluck or picnic – just carry the toasted nuts along separately and toss them with the rest of the salad right before serving.*

1. Combine all ingredients for the dressing and shake well.

2. Slice cabbage in quarters and cut away core. Slice into the finest shreds you can, or use a grater. Coarsely grate the carrots. Toss cabbage and carrots together with the green onions and raisins.

3. A few hours before serving, add parsley, toss salad with dressing, and refrigerate. At serving time, bring salad to room temperature, add toasted nuts, and enjoy.

Serves 6–8.

TIP:
• You can make the dressing and prepare the salad ingredients a day or two ahead. Store separately in covered containers in the refrigerator.

Asian Chicken
with Oriental Coleslaw or Oriental Noodle Salad

Asian Poached Chicken

1 cup	dry white wine	250 ml
1 stalk	lemon grass	
	or	
4 strips	lemon zest	
2 slices	fresh ginger root *(½" /1 cm thick), crushed*	
4 cloves	garlic, *crushed*	
4 sprigs	fresh coriander *or* parsley	
10	black peppercorns	
4	boneless chicken breasts	

Oriental Dressing

2 cloves	garlic, *minced*	
1 tsp	ginger, *grated*	5 ml
¼ cup	orange juice	60 ml
¼ cup	soy sauce	60 ml
1 tsp	sugar	5 ml
½ cup	vegetable oil	125 ml
1 tbsp	sesame oil	15 ml
1–2 tsp	red chili paste	5–10 ml
	freshly ground black pepper	

• *Chicken poached with oriental flavourings is the star in these two main-dish salads – one built on shredded cabbage, the other on rice vermicelli noodles. Either makes a great cold dinner on a hot summer night.*

Asian Poached Chicken

1. Combine all the ingredients except the chicken in a deep frying pan. Add 1 cup (250 ml) water. Bring to a boil, lower heat, and simmer for 5 minutes.

2. Add chicken, cover, and cook gently, turning once, for about 10 minutes – until chicken is tender and cooked through. Remove to a side dish, allow to cool, season with salt and pepper, and slice. Refrigerate until needed.

Oriental Dressing

1. Whisk together all the ingredients for the dressing. (Or combine in a food processor, slowly adding the oil last with the motor running.) Taste and adjust seasoning.

Makes about 1 cup (250 ml).

Please turn to next page for directions for Oriental Coleslaw and Oriental Noodle Salad

For one dinner, toss flavourful Asian Poached Chicken with rice noodles and vegetables; for another, arrange it on a bed of Oriental Coleslaw.

Oriental Coleslaw

½	small green cabbage	
2	large carrots	
½	red pepper	
½	green pepper	
8 ears	baby corn	
2 stalks	celery	
6	green onions	
½ cup	fresh parsley	125 ml
½ cup	Oriental Dressing	125 ml
½ cup	sliced almonds, *toasted, or* **rice crackers,** *crushed*	125 ml

Oriental Noodle Salad

½ lb	rice vermicelli noodles	250 g
2 cups	snow peas	500 ml
1	red pepper	
1	green pepper	
½	medium red onion	
½ cup	Oriental Dressing	125 ml
	fresh parsley *or* coriander *(optional)*	

Oriental Coleslaw

1. Finely shred the cabbage, julienne the carrots, and cut the peppers into slivers. Halve the baby corn lengthwise and thinly slice the celery on the diagonal. Chop the green onions and parsley.

2. In a large bowl, combine all the vegetables except the parsley and toss with Oriental Dressing. Arrange vegetables on a platter and top with the sliced Asian Poached Chicken. Sprinkle with parsley and almonds or crumbled rice crackers.

Serves 6–8.

Oriental Noodle Salad

1. Cook vermicelli noodles according to package directions. Toss with a little of the dressing. Chill.

2. Cut the snow peas and peppers into strips and thinly slice the onion.

3. To serve, toss noodles with sliced Asian Poached Chicken, snow peas, pepper strips, red onion, and enough dressing to thoroughly coat noodles. Garnish with chopped parsley or coriander if desired.

Serves 4–6.

TIPS:

• The Oriental Dressing keeps well in a covered jar in the refrigerator for 2–3 weeks.

• Look for red chili paste in the oriental-food section of the supermarket. Sambal oelek, an Indonesian/Malaysian chili mixture, is a good choice. Adjust the amount you add to suit your taste. If you prefer, you can substitute 1 tsp (5 ml) red chili flakes for the paste.

Mango Salsa

1	**ripe mango,** *peeled and diced*	
1	**small red onion,** *finely chopped*	
½	**jalapeño pepper,** *seeded and finely chopped*	
2 tbsp	**fresh coriander,** *chopped*	30 ml
2 tbsp	**lime juice**	30 ml
	salt and freshly ground black pepper	

TIPS:

• The salsa will keep nicely in the refrigerator for a couple of days.

• Mangoes are available in most large supermarkets and fruit markets. Choose ones with a sweet fragrance that are firm (but not hard) and unblemished. (If the mango is over-ripe, it will disintegrate in your salad.)

•Mangoes have a long, flattish pit in the centre, and the flesh doesn't pull away from it (as it does, say, from a peach pit). Follow the drawings for easy cutting – and to eat the sweet juicy mango chunks right off the peel.

• *This spicy relish goes nicely with grilled pork, fish, and chicken. (It's a great accompaniment to the Crispy Corn Chicken on p. 98.) Adjust the amount of jalapeño pepper to suit your taste.*

1. Combine ingredients, cover, and refrigerate. Bring to room temperature before serving.

Makes 1½ cups (375 ml).

PINEAPPLE SALSA:

• Substitute a ripe pineapple for the mango, chopped roasted red pepper for the jalapeño, and mint for the coriander. Add ¼ cup (60 ml) chopped parsley. This salsa goes particularly well with pork.

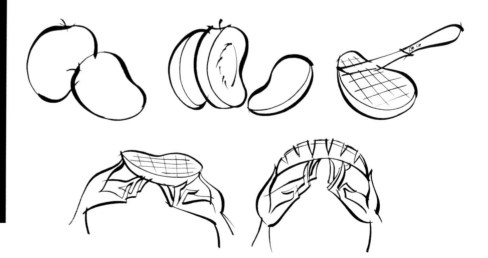

(Pineapple Salsa is shown in the photo opposite p. 44.)

Very, Very Green Salad

1 head	**broccoli,** *florets only*	
1½ cups	**green beans,** *sliced diagonally*	375 ml
1½ cups	**snow peas**	375 ml
1 bunch	**fresh spinach,** *trimmed, washed, and dried*	
1½ cups	**seedless green grapes**	375 ml
2 tbsp	**green onion,** *chopped*	30 ml
2 tbsp	**chives,** *chopped*	30 ml
½ cup	**golden raisins**	125 ml
½ lb	**bacon,** *cooked crisp and chopped (optional)*	250 g
½ cup	**pine nuts,** *toasted*	125 ml
2 cups	**Creamy Citrus Dressing** (p. 91)	500 ml

• *Beautiful colour, great taste – plus, it serves a crowd. This salad goes well with Pepper-Encrusted Loin of Pork (p. 44) or simply grilled chicken.*

1. Combine all ingredients except dressing, bacon (if using), and pine nuts in a large bowl. Toss to mix well.

2. Add Creamy Citrus Dressing and toss again. Chill 1 hour before serving to let flavours blend.

3. Just before serving, add pine nuts and bacon (optional) and toss again.

Serves 10.

TIP:

•Blanching the broccoli, beans, and snow peas for 1–2 minutes in lightly salted boiling water brings out their flavour and colour. Use the same pot, putting in one type of vegetable at a time. Lift out with a slotted spoon, refresh in ice water to stop the cooking, and drain thoroughly.

Very, Very Green Salad: You can vary the green items to suit your own taste (and the contents of your fridge).

Wild Rice Salad
with Fruit & Nuts

1 cup	wild rice	250 ml
½ cup	basmati *or* **long-grain white rice**	125 ml
1	orange	
½ cup	dried cranberries	125 ml
4	green onions	
½ cup	pecans, *toasted and chopped*	125 ml
¼ cup	fresh parsley, *chopped*	60 ml
½ cup	Citrus Vinaigrette *(facing page)*	125 ml
	salt and freshly ground black pepper	

TIP:

• Basmati rice should be rinsed before using to remove surface dust. Put the rice in a bowl, pour in cold water, and swirl grains around with your fingers. Pour off the water and repeat till the water runs clear. Before steaming basmati, cover with fresh, cold water, and leave to soak for 15–30 minutes. Drain and cook.

• *Delicious nutty flavours and satisfying crunch. This salad goes well with grilled chicken or pork marinated in the same Citrus Vinaigrette (facing page).*

1. Place wild rice in a large saucepan, cover with 4 cups (1 L) water, and add a dash of salt. Bring to a boil, lower heat, cover, and simmer until grains are tender but still chewy, about 30 minutes.

2. Bring 4 cups (1 L) water to a boil. Add basmati or white rice. Boil for about 10 minutes until grains are just tender. Drain.

3. While rice is still warm, toss both types together with half the dressing and set aside.

4. Cut the skin and pith from the orange. Slice the orange, then cut each slice into bite-sized pieces. Soak the dried cranberries in warm water or orange juice for 15 minutes to soften. Drain and pat dry.

5. Shortly before serving, add the fruit, green onions, nuts, and parsley to the rice. Toss with more of the dressing and season to taste.

Serves 4–6.

TIPS:

• You can substitute golden raisins for the cranberries, or 1 cup (250 ml) of seedless purple or red grapes, cut in half.

• The rice can be cooked and combined with the dressing (Steps 1–3), and the other ingredients prepared (Step 4), early in the day. Toss all together just before serving.

Two Citrus Dressings

• Use the Creamy Citrus Dressing on the Very, Very Green Salad, p. 88; the Citrus Vinaigrette, on the Wild Rice Salad, facing page.

Creamy Citrus Dressing

1 cup	mayonnaise	250 ml
½ cup	orange juice	125 ml
2 tsp	honey	10 ml
½ cup	sour cream *or* yogurt	125 ml
1 tbsp	rice vinegar	15 ml
1 tsp	dry mustard	5 ml
1 clove	garlic, *minced*	
2	green onions, *chopped*	
¼ cup	parsley, *chopped*	60 ml
1 tsp	salt	5 ml
1 tsp	dry mustard	5 ml
	salt and freshly ground black pepper	

1. Combine all ingredients, mixing well, and season to taste. (Dressing can be made in a food processor if desired.) Keep refrigerated until ready to use. *Makes about 2 cups (500 ml).*

Citrus Vinaigrette

1 tbsp	orange juice	15 ml
1 tbsp	lemon juice	15 ml
1 tbsp	balsamic *or* red wine vinegar	15 ml
6 tbsp	olive oil	90 ml
	salt and freshly ground black pepper	

1. Whisk all the dressing ingredients together. *Makes about ½ cup (125 ml).*

TIPS:

• Rice vinegar has a mild, sweet taste that is well suited to the creamy dressing. However, you can substitute another white vinegar if desired.

• The Citrus Vinaigrette makes a good marinade for chicken or pork.

WATERCRESS & ORANGE SALAD:

• Toss most of the Citrus Vinaigrette with 6 cups (1.5 L) watercress; ½ small red onion, thinly sliced; 2 green onions or 1 shallot, minced; and 1 large orange, peeled and cut into bite-sized pieces. Add a little more dressing if necessary. A piece of Stilton crumbled on top is a delicious accompaniment.

Pickled Beets with a Bite

1 lb	beets	500 g
1 tsp	creamed horseradish	5 ml
1 tbsp	white wine vinegar	15 ml
2 tbsp	vegetable oil	30 ml
	fresh dill *or* parsley, *chopped* (optional)	
	salt and freshly ground black pepper	

TIP:

• The pickled beets will keep for several days in the refrigerator.

QUICK TRICK:

For a salad with great colour and flavour, toss equal quantities of grated raw beets and grated raw carrots with a simple dressing of two parts oil, one part lemon juice, and salt and pepper.

• *The beet is experiencing a renaissance. Small, summer-fresh ones are especially sweet. Try mild golden beets or, for a treat, splurge on an orangey-red variety called Chiogga, whose flesh has dramatic red and white rings.*

1. Cut away all but 1" (2.5 cm) of the leafy tops from the beets, leaving the skin and tail intact, and scrub clean. Wrap in foil and bake in a 350°F (180°C) oven until tender. Test after 30 minutes; cooking time will depend on the freshness and size of the beets. Trim away the tops and tails, and remove the skin. Slice beets and cut into $1/2$" (1.25 cm) cubes.

2. Combine remaining ingredients and toss with beets.

3. Cover and chill for a few hours before serving.

Makes about 2 cups (500 ml).

MORE PICKLED PRODUCE:

• Make up a batch of Pickled Cucumbers to keep in the fridge – they'll last a week. Score an English cucumber lengthwise with the tines of a fork and slice wafer thin. Lay the slices on a plate, sprinkle with salt, cover with plastic, and weight down. Leave for an hour, then drain away the liquid. Cover the slices with a mixture of $1/2$ cup (125 ml) white wine vinegar, 2 tbsp (30 ml) each of sugar and fresh chopped dill, and some salt and pepper. Chill for several hours before serving.

Spinach Rice

1 lb	**fresh spinach**	500 g
3 tbsp	**olive oil**	45 ml
1	**large onion,** *finely chopped*	
1 clove	**garlic,** *finely chopped*	
1 cup	**medium-grain** *or* **arborio rice**	250 ml
½ cup	**fresh dill,** *chopped*	125 ml
½ cup	**fresh parsley,** *chopped*	125 ml
1	**lemon,** *juice and grated zest*	
1½ cups	**water** *or* **chicken stock**	375 ml
	salt and freshly ground black pepper	

• *A side dish with the flavour of the Greek islands. Medium-grain or arborio rice combined with the light, fresh tastes of dill and lemon makes a tasty accompaniment to grilled chicken, Skewered Fish (p. 62), or Cumin-Scented Leg of Lamb (p. 65). The same combination, perhaps with the addition of a little crumbled feta cheese, is an ideal stuffing for tomatoes.*

1. Trim tough stalks off spinach and blanch leaves for 2 minutes in a large pot of lightly salted boiling water. Drain. Immerse spinach in ice water to stop the cooking and drain again. Squeeze dry and chop roughly. Set aside.

2. Heat oil in a 3 qt (3 L) heavy-bottomed saucepan. Add onion and cook until soft. Add spinach; garlic; rice; about ¾ of the dill, parsley, lemon juice and lemon zest; ½ tsp (2 ml) salt; and a few turns of the pepper mill. Stir for a couple of minutes until rice grains are coated with flavoured oil.

3. Add water or stock, stir gently, and bring to a boil. Cover pot, reduce heat to low, and cook gently for 15 minutes.

4. Remove pan from heat. Set aside, covered, for 10 minutes. Serve warm, sprinkled with remaining dill, parsley, lemon juice, and lemon zest.

Serves 4.

Lentil & Olive Salad

2½ cups	cooked green lentils *(2-19 oz/540 ml cans)*	625 ml
½ cup	Greek olives, *pitted*	125 ml
2 tbsp	capers, *rinsed*	30 ml
1	anchovy fillet, *rinsed (optional)*	
1 clove	garlic, *minced*	
2 tbsp	fresh lemon juice	30 ml
¼ cup	olive oil	60 ml
1 tbsp	fresh oregano, *chopped* or	15 ml
1 tsp	dried oregano	5 ml
	salt and freshly ground black pepper	
2 tbsp	fresh Italian (flat-leaf) parsley, *chopped*	30 ml
2 tbsp	onion, *finely chopped*	30 ml

TIP:

• This salad tastes even better after it has sat in the refrigerator for a few hours and the flavours have had a chance to blend.

• An easy, Mediterranean-flavoured make-ahead salad that consists mostly of ingredients from the cupboard.

1. By hand or using a blender or food processor, finely chop the olives, capers, anchovy fillet, and garlic, and combine with the lemon juice, olive oil, and oregano; season to taste.

2. If you are using canned lentils, rinse them well. Toss lentils with part of the olive dressing and set aside.

3. Before serving, toss salad, adding more dressing and adjusting seasoning. Scatter chopped onion, parsley, and a few extra whole olives on top.

Serves 4–6.

TIP:

• 1 cup dried lentils equals 2½ cups cooked. To cook dried lentils, pick them over to remove stones and debris, and rinse. Toss into a large quantity of salted water, along with a bay leaf and the leaves from a stalk of celery. Bring to a boil and cook over moderate heat until just tender. Cooking time varies – start testing the lentils after 20 minutes so you don't overcook. Drain and rinse under cold water. Remove herbs.

Saffron Rice Pilaf

3 cups	fish stock *or* **light chicken stock**	750 ml
½ tsp	saffron threads	2 ml
2 tbsp	olive oil	30 ml
1 cup	Spanish onion, *finely chopped*	250 ml
2–3 cloves	garlic, *minced*	
½	red pepper, *seeded and chopped*	
½	green pepper, *seeded and chopped*	
2	ripe plum tomatoes, *peeled, seeded, and chopped*	
1½ cups	medium-grain Spanish rice *or* **arborio rice**	375 ml
	salt and freshly ground black pepper	
	lemon slices and fresh parsley, *chopped (for garnish)*	

• *This fragrant, golden rice is essential for Lazy Summer Paella (p. 41). It's also delicious under Skewered Fish (p. 62) or simple grilled lamb or pork.*

1. Heat stock in a small saucepan. Cook saffron in a small dry frying pan over moderate heat for about 30 seconds to bring out the flavour.

2. Pour half a cup of stock from the saucepan into a small bowl, crumble the toasted saffron into the hot liquid, and set aside to steep.

3. Heat oil in a large, deep frying pan with a well-fitting lid. Add onion and cook over moderate heat until soft, then add garlic, peppers, and tomatoes, and continue to cook for about 10 minutes. Add rice and stir over the heat for a few minutes until all the grains are coated with the flavoured oil.

4. Pour in the hot stock and the saffron-flavoured liquid and stir gently while mixture comes to a boil. Reduce the heat to low, cover, and leave to cook for about 15 minutes, until liquid is absorbed and rice is tender. Remove from heat and set aside, covered, for about 5 minutes.

5. Fluff the rice with a fork, season, and turn out onto a warm platter. Garnish with parsley and lemon slices and serve.

Serves 6.

IV. MAKE-AHEAD MAIN DISHES, PASTAS, & ONE-POT MEALS

CONTENTS

QUICK TRICKS

IN OTHER CHAPTERS...

Sauce Solutions

The following recipes in other sections of the book also make great — and very quick — toppings for pasta.

Slow-Roasted Garlic Chicken (p. 100)

MEATLESS MAIN DISH

* These recipes are meatless, or have a meatless option

CROWD PLEASERS

Meatless Entertaining (for 4)

Baked Brie with Sun-Dried Tomato Pesto (*pp. 14 and 25*) **and garlic toasts**

Mushroom Ragout over Pasta or Polenta (*p. 103*)

Steamed asparagus or green beans

Arugula Orange Salad (*p. 71*)

Totally Decadent Rice Pudding with Strawberry Rhubarb Compote (*pp. 184 and 162*)

Make-Ahead, Take-Along Supper or Picnic Lunch (for 8)

Crispy Corn Chicken (*p. 98*) **with Mango Salsa** (*p. 87*) (*double the recipes*)

Chickpeas & Roasted Peppers (*p. 81*) (*double the recipe*)

Red Cabbage Salad (*p. 83*)

Couldn't-Be-Easier Chocolate Banana Cake (*p. 156*)

Dress Up Your Tomato Sauce

A good tomato sauce (*p. 110*) opens many possibilities. For a quick dinner, add one or more of these to the sauce, heat gently, and serve over pasta:

- sliced kalamata olives
- chopped sun-dried tomatoes
- dried porcini mushrooms, soaked and drained
- lightly browned sautéed sliced fresh mushrooms
- roasted red peppers
- a variety of diced roasted or sautéed vegetables, such as eggplant, peppers, zucchini, fennel, and onions

- chunks of browned sweet or hot Italian sausage
- sliced boneless chicken (heat the sauce in the same pan in which you sauté the chicken, deglazing it with a little wine before adding the sauce)
- also try the following recipes, which start with tomato sauce: Braised Pork (*p. 112*), Shrimp with Feta (*p. 111*), Penne with Italian Sausage (*p. 114*), Clams or Mussels in Red Sauce (*p. 111*).

MORE SUMMER WEEKENDS

Crispy Corn Chicken
with Mango Salsa

8	chicken pieces	
1 clove	garlic, *minced*	
2	eggs	
2 tbsp	butter	30 ml
¼ cup	olive oil	60 ml
¾ cup	cornmeal	175 ml
¼ cup	Parmesan cheese, *grated*	60 ml
1 tsp	dried oregano	5 ml
	salt and freshly ground black pepper	

TIP:

• If you're making the chicken ahead, set the cooked pieces on paper towel on a rack to cool, then wrap in foil and store in the refrigerator.

VARIATION:

• Kids will love Crispy Corn Chicken Fingers: Pound boneless chicken breasts to flatten and cut into strips. Proceed with the recipe as above, except reduce cooking time to 10 minutes on one side, 5 minutes on the other, then a final 5 minutes after spooning away excess fat.

• *Delicious cold or hot and easily made ahead, these chicken pieces are great for a quick supper. (If you make a double batch, you'll have some on hand for lunch or to pack into a picnic basket.) You can use a whole chicken cut up or just thighs and legs, which are easy to eat with your fingers. Mango Salsa (p. 87) is a tasty condiment to serve alongside, but chili sauce or fruit chutney would also be good.*

1. Mash garlic with a little salt, add to eggs with some pepper, and beat to combine. Pour mixture over chicken pieces, coating them on all sides.

2. Set butter and oil in a large, shallow roasting pan in a 350°F (180°C) oven to preheat.

3. Combine cornmeal, Parmesan cheese, oregano, salt, and pepper on a plate. Roll the chicken pieces one at a time in the cornmeal mixture, patting on the coating to make an even layer. Set aside on paper towel.

4. Add chicken pieces to the preheated pan, basting on all sides with the hot oil. Cook for 20 minutes. Turn, baste, and cook for 15 minutes longer. Spoon away excess fat from pan and turn the chicken pieces again, cooking for 10–15 minutes more (5–10 minutes for the white meat) until the juices run clear when tested and the outside is crispy and nicely browned. Drain on paper towel. Enjoy hot or cold.

Serves 4.

Very Lemon Chicken

1 clove	**garlic,** *halved*	
¼ cup	**extra-virgin olive oil**	**60 ml**
½ cup	**fresh lemon juice**	**125 ml**
1	**small onion,** *grated*	
1 tsp	**dried thyme**	**5 ml**
1	**fresh hot pepper,** *seeded and chopped*	
2 tbsp	**butter** *or* **olive oil**	**30 ml**
6	**boneless, skinless chicken breast halves**	
	salt and freshly ground black pepper	

• *A quick and easy dish to put together. When doubled, it feeds a large group, and there are many ways to use leftovers. (The chicken is excellent cold, shredded for a wrap or sliced in a sandwich; see p. 127.) The chicken pieces can be cooked ahead of time. Reheat and serve over rice or with crispy roasted potatoes and crunchy green beans or fresh asparagus for a complete supper, or with salad and warm biscuits for a lighter evening meal.*

1. Combine the garlic, olive oil, lemon juice, onion, thyme, and hot pepper in a small bowl. Cover and leave in the refrigerator for an hour or so while the flavours blend.

2. Heat the butter or oil in a large frying pan. Season the chicken breasts and lightly brown on both sides. (You may have to cook them in two batches so as not to crowd the pan.)

3. Pour lemon mixture over the chicken and cover the pan. Lower heat and simmer until chicken is cooked, about 10 minutes, depending on the size of the breasts.

Serves 6.

QUICK TRICK:

A good ready-to-go curry paste – see p. 9 for a buying tip – can be used to make an excellent chicken, vegetable, or meat curry on the spur of the moment. Just follow the directions on the jar or package. Steam some rice, open a jar of chutney, and you'll have dinner on the table in no time at all. If you're looking for a vegetarian idea, potatoes and chickpeas make a great curry combo.

Slow-Roasted Garlic Chicken

3 lbs	chicken pieces	1.5 kg
1	large onion, *cut in eighths*	
2 heads	garlic, *separated into cloves (about 20 unpeeled cloves)*	
1 tsp	dried rosemary *or* tarragon	5 ml
½	lemon, *thinly sliced*	
2 tbsp	olive oil	30 ml
1 cup	fruity white wine	250 ml
	salt and freshly ground black pepper	

TIPS:

• The softened garlic cloves can be squeezed out of their skins and eaten as is with the meat or spread onto bread. You can also blend some of the garlic into the sauce or mash it with the potatoes.

• If you're making the dish ahead, complete through Step 4. Then simply reheat in a covered casserole in a 350°F (180°C) oven.

• *This recipe takes just a few minutes to put together and reheats well. The quantity of garlic may seem outrageous, but slow roasting softens and sweetens its flavour. Serve the chicken with a platter of lightly steamed green beans, Olive-Flavoured Mashed Potatoes (Quick Trick, below), and warm, crusty bread.*

1. Toss chicken pieces in a bowl with the onion, garlic, herbs, lemon slices, olive oil, salt, and pepper.

2. Place the chicken in a shallow roasting pan, scatter the onion, garlic, and lemon slices over and around it, and sprinkle with the wine.

3. Cover the pan tightly with foil and place on the centre rack of a preheated 350°F (180°C) oven. After about an hour, remove foil, baste chicken with the pan juices and continue to roast, uncovered, until the chicken is lightly browned and cooked through – about 20 minutes more.

4. Transfer chicken and garlic cloves from the pan to a serving dish. Strain the cooking juices into a small saucepan, skim off fat, and simmer for a few minutes to strengthen the flavour. Season to taste and pour over the chicken.

Serves 4.

QUICK TRICK:

Olive-Flavoured Mashed Potatoes: Into mashed potatoes for 4, fold ½ cup (125 ml) coarsely chopped Niçoise olives and ¼–⅓ cup (60–75 ml) warm olive oil. Season to taste.

You'll want to serve this Slow-Roasted Garlic Chicken with warm bread, so people can smear the sweet cloves of garlic on it like soft butter.

Lisa Olsson's Meatballs

1 cup	beef stock	250 ml
2 slices	white bread	
1 lb	ground beef	500 g
1 lb	ground pork	500 g
1	large boiled potato, *peeled and mashed*	
¼ cup	18% cream	60 ml
½ cup	Cheddar cheese, *grated*	125 ml
1½ tsp	baking powder	7 ml
1	large onion, *peeled and grated*	
2	egg yolks	
1 tbsp each butter and oil		15 ml
	salt and freshly ground black pepper	

Sauce

1 cup	beef stock	250 ml
½ cup	18% cream	125 ml
2 tbsp	lingonberry sauce, grape jelly, *or* cranberry sauce	30 ml

• *Swedish meatballs are such a well-known buffet dish that they're almost a cliché. Don't let that reputation deter you from trying this recipe, which comes from a friend who grew up in Sweden. The sauce is sweetened with berries, the meatballs are light and tender, and the result is deliciously different. Serve over wide egg noodles as a main dish, or by themselves as a party appetizer.*

1. Remove crusts from bread and soak slices in stock until soft. Squeeze dry.

2. Combine bread with all the other meatball ingredients except the butter and oil, blending well to form a smooth, light mixture. Form into small balls, about 1" (2.5 cm) in diameter.

3. Heat butter and oil in a large, heavy frying pan. Fry the meatballs, about a dozen at a time, over medium-high heat. Turn them frequently until well browned on all sides, about 7–8 minutes. Keep the cooked meatballs warm while you make the sauce.

4. Pour away the cooking fat from the pan. Add stock and table cream, and set the pan over high heat, scraping up all the crispy brown bits stuck to the bottom. Reduce the sauce until slightly thickened, season to taste, and swirl in the lingonberry sauce, grape jelly, or cranberry sauce. Pour sauce over meatballs and serve immediately.

Makes about 60 meatballs.

TIP:
• The meatballs can be made ahead and gently reheated in the sauce.

Mushroom Ragout
over Pasta or Polenta

2–3 tbsp	olive oil	30–45 ml
½ lb	**portobello mushroom caps,** *thinly sliced*	250 g
1 lb	**white mushrooms,** *sliced*	500 g
1	**medium onion,** *finely chopped*	
2 cloves	**garlic,** *finely chopped*	
1 tsp	**fresh rosemary** *or* **tarragon,** *chopped* *or*	5 ml
½ tsp	**dried rosemary** *or* **tarragon**	2 ml
pinch	**red pepper flakes**	
½ cup	**vegetable stock**	125 ml
1 tbsp	**balsamic vinegar**	15 ml
¼ cup	**fresh parsley,** *chopped*	60 ml
	salt and freshly ground black pepper	
	Parmesan cheese, *grated*	

• *Portobello mushrooms give this versatile (and quick-to-put-together) dish a rich, robust flavour and an almost meaty texture. (It's a popular main course even among diehard meat-eaters.)*

1. Heat half the oil in a large, heavy frying pan over medium-high heat. Add half the mushrooms and cook, tossing over the heat until lightly browned and almost tender. Season, scrape into a bowl, and set aside. Repeat with the remaining mushrooms, adding a little more oil to the pan if necessary.

2. Heat remaining oil in the pan, add onion, and cook until soft and lightly browned, about 10 minutes. Add garlic, herbs, pepper flakes, and seasoning and cook for 2–3 minutes before stirring in the stock.

3. Return mushrooms and any collected juices to the pan. Stir all together, lower heat, and simmer for a couple of minutes to blend flavours. Taste, adjust seasoning, and add a splash of vinegar to sharpen the flavour. Serve hot over pasta or polenta (see Tip, below) with a garnish of fresh chopped parsley and grated Parmesan.

Serves 4.

VARIATION:

• **The mushroom mixture could also be served over rice, baked under a puff pastry crust, or used as a filling for omelettes.**

TIP:

• **To make polenta to serve with stews and sauces, follow the recipe on p. 28 through Step 2, but use 1 part cornmeal to 4 parts water so the polenta is softer and creamier.**

Provençal Lamb Stew
with White Beans & Rosemary

1½ lbs	**lean lamb,** *cubed*	**750 g**
2 tbsp	**olive oil**	**30 ml**
1 tbsp	**flour**	**15 ml**
2	**onions,** *chopped*	
2 cloves	**garlic,** *minced*	
1	**carrot,** *chopped*	
1	**celery stalk,** *chopped*	
1 cup	**dry white wine**	**250 ml**
1 cup	**chicken stock**	**250 ml**
1 can	**plum tomatoes,** *drained and chopped* (28 oz/796 ml)	
1 tbsp	**fresh rosemary,** *chopped* **or**	**15 ml**
1 tsp	**dried rosemary**	**5 ml**
1	**bay leaf**	
1 can	**white beans,** *rinsed and drained* (19 oz/540 ml)	
	fresh parsley, *chopped*	
	salt and freshly ground black pepper	

• *This stew is full of the flavours of southern France and tastes even better if made a day ahead of serving. Accompany with mounds of garlicky mashed potatoes and a simple steamed green vegetable.*

1. Heat oil in a large, heavy frying pan. Add lamb cubes in small batches and brown well on all sides. Use a slotted spoon to transfer the browned lamb to a flameproof casserole. Sprinkle with flour, season lightly, and toss over high heat for a couple of minutes.

2. Meanwhile, add onions, garlic, carrot, and celery to the frying pan (you may need to add a dash more oil) and cook over medium heat, stirring frequently, until onions are soft, about 5 minutes. Add wine and bring to a boil, scraping up all the good bits on the bottom.

3. Transfer vegetable mixture to the casserole and combine with the lamb. Add stock, tomatoes, and herbs.

4. Bring gently to a boil, lower heat, cover, and simmer until lamb is tender, about an hour, adding beans midway through the cooking time. Serve hot, sprinkled with parsley.

Serves 4.

VARIATION:

• Substitute cubes of lean pork or chunks of chicken for the lamb in this dish.

Hearty Provençal Lamb Stew is the perfect antidote to a cool, rainy day. A boned leg of lamb works well in this dish.

Shortcut Seafood Curry

1½–2 lbs	**mixed seafood 750 g–1 kg** *(shrimp, scallops, and firm-fleshed fish such as grouper, monkfish, or halibut)*	
1 tsp each	**garlic and fresh ginger,** *chopped*	5 ml
1	**small hot green chili,** *seeded and chopped*	
½	**lemon,** *grated rind and juice*	
1 tsp	**ground cumin**	5 ml
	freshly ground pepper	
4 tbsp	**vegetable oil**	60 ml
1	**medium onion,** *finely chopped*	
1 cup	**tomatoes** *(fresh or canned),* *chopped*	250 ml
1 cup	**coconut milk**	250 ml
	salt	
¼ cup	**fresh coriander** *or* **parsley,** *chopped*	60 ml

• *Coconut milk – available in cans in many supermarkets – gives this curry its richness and Indonesian/Thai flavour. This recipe calls for lemon rind and juice rather than the authentic but harder-to-find lemon grass. The preparation can be done in stages and the quantities doubled to make an excellent party dish. Serve over steamed basmati or coconut rice.*

1. Cut fish into 1½" (4 cm) cubes. (Leave shrimp and scallops whole.) Toss seafood with garlic, ginger, chili, lemon juice and rind, cumin and pepper. Set aside in the refrigerator for a few hours.

2. In a large frying pan, heat 2 tbsp (30 ml) of the oil, and cook the onion until golden. Add tomatoes. Cook, stirring occasionally, for 10 minutes.

3. Reduce heat to low and gently stir in coconut milk. (Do not overheat, as the coconut milk will curdle.) Simmer about 5 minutes to form a creamy sauce. Add salt to taste.

4. Just before you're ready to serve, heat remaining oil in a clean frying pan, add seafood mixture, and toss over medium heat for about 5 minutes, until seafood is just cooked through. (It is ready when the flesh turns from translucent to opaque.)

5. Combine seafood with sauce and gently heat, about 5 minutes. Season to taste. Serve over rice, garnished with chopped coriander or parsley.

Serves 4.

African Lamb Curry

2 tbsp	vegetable oil	30 ml
1	medium onion, *finely chopped*	
4–6 cloves	garlic, *finely chopped*	
1 tbsp	curry powder	15 ml
½ tsp	ground cumin	2 ml
1–2	small hot dried chili(es)	
2 lbs	lean lamb, *cut in cubes*	1 kg
2 cups	tomatoes, *(fresh or canned),* *chopped*	500 ml
1	sweet potato, *peeled and diced*	
1	potato, *peeled and diced*	
2 tbsp	crunchy peanut butter	30 ml
	salt	

• Curries are well suited to being made ahead, as this gives the flavour time to develop. The inclusion in this one of sweet potatoes and peanuts – in the convenient form of crunchy peanut butter – reveals its African roots. Serve with steamed rice, a fruit chutney, and some additional chopped roasted peanuts to sprinkle on top.

1. Heat oil in a large pot, add onion and garlic, and cook over medium heat until soft.

2. Sprinkle in curry powder, cumin, and chili(es); stir for a few seconds. Then toss in lamb cubes and cook for about 5 minutes.

3. Add tomatoes, sweet potato, and potato. Bring to a boil, then lower heat, cover, and simmer until meat is tender – about 1–1½ hours. Add a little water (or stock) if the mixture seems to be getting too dry.

4. Stir in peanut butter and add salt to taste.

Serves 4–6.

VARIATION:

• For a vegetarian version, omit the lamb and add 4 cups (1 L) of other vegetables, such as eggplant, green beans, green or yellow squash, peppers, carrots, and celery. Add hard vegetables first and soft ones later, so they all become tender at the same time.

North African Chicken Stew

1½ lbs	**boned chicken pieces,** *cut in 1½" (4 cm) chunks*	**750 g**
3 tbsp	**lemon juice**	**45 ml**
1 tsp	**ground cumin**	**5 ml**
½ tsp	**ground allspice**	**2 ml**
½ tsp	**cayenne**	**2 ml**
2 tbsp	**olive oil**	**30 ml**
1	**medium red onion,** *chopped*	
2 cloves	**garlic,** *minced*	
4	**green onions,** *chopped*	
1	**butternut or other squash,** *peeled, seeded, and cubed*	
2 cups	**chicken stock**	**500 ml**
1 can	**chickpeas,** *rinsed and drained* (19 oz/540 ml)	
	fresh coriander *or* **parsley,** *chopped*	
1	**lemon,** *sliced*	
	salt and freshly ground black pepper	

• *Accompanied by some warm flatbread to mop up the savoury sauce, this stew is a complete meal in a dish. It can be prepared in just half an hour, and if there is any left over, it's good reheated the next day. You can use either thighs or breasts, or a combination.*

1. In a bowl, combine chicken pieces with lemon juice and spices. Set aside.

2. Heat oil in a large, heavy frying pan or flameproof casserole. Add red onion, garlic, green onions, and squash and cook over medium heat, stirring frequently, for about 5 minutes.

3. Add spiced chicken pieces to the pot, season lightly, and toss over the heat for 2–3 minutes before adding the stock and chickpeas. Bring gently to a boil, lower heat, cover, and simmer until chicken is just cooked and vegetables are tender, about 10 minutes longer.

4. Serve hot, garnished with coriander or parsley and a lemon slice.

Serves 4.

Fresh Vegetable Stew
with Herbed Buttermilk Biscuit Topping

2 tbsp	**olive oil**	**30 ml**
1 tbsp	**butter**	**15 ml**
3	**leeks, white part only,** *chopped*	
4 cups	**assorted vegetables,** *(see Variations, below), chopped according to length of cooking time required*	**1 L**
2	**plum tomatoes** *(fresh or canned), seeded and chopped*	
2 cloves	**garlic,** *minced*	
1 tsp	**dried thyme**	**5 ml**
1 tbsp	**flour**	**15 ml**
3 cups	**vegetable stock** *or* **water**	**750 ml**
¼ cup	**fresh parsley,** *chopped*	**60 ml**
1 tbsp	**fresh basil,** *chopped*	**15 ml**
	dough for Herbed Buttermilk Biscuits *(p. 133)*	
	salt and freshly ground black pepper	

• *A great vegetarian main dish. Vary the vegetables and herbs to take advantage of what's in season. The stew can be prepared through Step 3 a day ahead.*

1. Heat oil and butter in a large, heavy pot over medium heat. Add leeks and cook until soft, about 10 minutes.

2. Stir in chopped vegetables, tomatoes, garlic, and thyme. Cook 5 minutes.

3. Sprinkle with flour and toss over heat for a few minutes. Stir in stock (or water) and salt and pepper. Bring to a boil, lower heat, and simmer, partially covered, until vegetables are tender, about 30 minutes. Stir in fresh herbs.

4. When ready to serve, spoon vegetables into a 9" x 13" (23 cm x 33 cm) shallow baking dish. Drop spoonfuls of biscuit mixture on top and bake in preheated 425°F (220°C) oven for 15–20 minutes until stew is bubbling and topping is lightly browned.

Serves 6.

VARIATIONS:

• Vegetable combination #1: carrots, waxy potatoes, white turnips, green beans, and summer squash

• Vegetable combination #2: fresh peas, yellow zucchini, asparagus, and red peppers, with fresh thyme

• Vegetable combination #3: carrots, butternut squash, celery, red peppers, and mushrooms, with fresh rosemary

Roasted Plum Tomato Sauce

4½ lbs	fresh ripe plum tomatoes	2.5 kg
¼ cup	olive oil	60 ml
1	large onion, *thinly sliced*	
2 cloves	garlic, *slivered*	
1 tbsp	fresh thyme sprigs *or*	15 ml
2 tsp	dried thyme *or* oregano	10 ml
	salt and freshly ground black pepper	

QUICK TRICK:

Meatballs and spaghetti is a great feed-a-crowd dish. For tender meatballs, don't fry them at all – just simmer them in your sauce, where they will soak up the taste of the tomatoes and herbs. Combine 1½ lbs (750 g) ground beef (or a mixture of ground pork, veal, and beef), an egg beaten into ¼ cup (60 ml) water, ¼ cup (60 ml) Parmesan cheese, ½ cup (125 ml) fresh bread crumbs, 1 tsp (5 ml) oregano, and a small grated onion. This will make at least a dozen 2" (5 cm) meatballs. If you happen to have any left over, they make a delectable, messy sandwich.

• *A good tomato sauce provides the foundation for a number of easy meals. By combining it with special ingredients, such as pork tenderloin (p. 112) or shrimp (facing page), it becomes an elegant, crowd-dazzling dish. This sauce is prepared partly on the barbecue, and the charred tomato skins give it a rich sweetness.*

1. Toss whole tomatoes in a large bowl with half the oil. Set tomatoes on a very hot grill or under the broiler and cook, turning frequently, until the skins are blistered and charred, about 5 minutes. Purée in the food processor.

2. Heat the remaining oil in a large skillet. Add onion, garlic, and herbs and cook gently until soft.

3. Add the pureéd charred tomatoes and cook, stirring frequently, until sauce is thickened to your liking, about 5–10 minutes. Season with salt and pepper. Store in the refrigerator or freezer.

Makes about 4½ cups (1.25 L).

Shrimp with Feta
& Roasted Plum Tomato Sauce

4 cups	**Roasted Plum Tomato Sauce** *(facing page)* or **other good tomato sauce**	1 L
1 cup	**dry white wine**	250 ml
1 lb	**large raw shrimp,** *peeled and deveined*	500 g
4 oz	**feta cheese,** *crumbled*	125 g
	salt and freshly ground black pepper	
	fresh parsley, *chopped*	

• *A simplified version of a favourite Greek meal, this dish takes just a couple of minutes to put together. Serve over Saffron Rice (p. 95) with lots of fresh parsley.*

1. In a large, heavy pot, simmer the tomato sauce and wine together for a few minutes.

2. Add shrimp and simmer 5 minutes, then add crumbled feta and simmer for a few minutes more.

3. Taste and adjust seasoning. Sprinkle with parsley.

Serves 4.

QUICK TRICKS:

For a quick Red Clam Sauce, drain a 5 oz (142 g) can of clams, reserving ¼ cup (60 ml) juice. Heat the reserved juice with ½ cup (125 ml) white wine (optional) and reduce by half, then stir in 2 cups (500 ml) tomato sauce. Warm gently, then add clams, a pinch of thyme, and a dash of hot sauce, and simmer all together for 5 minutes. Serve over linguine. (The sauce can be prepared ahead.)

• Add steamed mussels (p. 18), either in the shell or out, and a little of their cooking broth to tomato sauce and serve over pasta, sprinkled with fresh chopped parsley.

Braised Pork
with Roasted Plum Tomato Sauce & Rosemary

2	**pork tenderloins,** *approx. 3/4 lb/375 g each*	
1/4 cup	**flour**	**60 ml**
	salt and freshly ground black pepper	
1 tsp	**paprika**	**5 ml**
2 tbsp	**olive oil**	**30 ml**
1/2 cup	**red wine** *or* **chicken stock**	**125 ml**
1 clove	**garlic,** *minced*	
2	**fresh rosemary sprigs** *or*	
1 tsp	**dried rosemary**	**5 ml**
1 1/2 cups	**Roasted Plum Tomato Sauce** *(p. 110) or* **other good tomato sauce**	**375 ml**
1/4 cup	**35% cream** *or* **chicken stock**	**60 ml**

• *This richly flavoured make-ahead dish is elegant enough to serve for a special dinner. Accompany with rice, roasted potatoes, or egg noodles; and grilled mixed peppers, roasted fennel, or steamed fresh green beans.*

1. Cut the pork tenderloins on the diagonal into 1/2" (1 cm) slices and pound to flatten.

2. Season flour with salt, pepper, and paprika, and dip each pork slice into the mixture, shaking off the excess.

3. In a large, heavy skillet, heat olive oil over medium-high heat. Add pork slices a few at a time and brown quickly on both sides. Set aside.

4. Add wine or stock to the pan with garlic and rosemary and bring to a boil, scraping up the browned bits on the bottom of the pan.

5. Stir in the tomato sauce and simmer for 5 minutes, then return the pork slices to the pan and continue to simmer gently until they are cooked through, about 5 more minutes.

6. Stir in cream or stock. Taste and adjust seasoning.

Serves 4.

TIP:

• The dish can be prepared through Step 5 a day or two ahead. Reheat gently, then stir in cream or stock.

A good tomato sauce does more than cover pasta. It can provide the foundation for an elegant dish, such as Braised Pork flavoured with rosemary.

Penne with Italian Sausage
& Roasted Tomato-Porcini Mushroom Sauce

2 oz	dried porcini mushrooms	50 g
1 tbsp	olive oil	15 ml
6	mild Italian sausages, *casings removed*	
1 cup	**Roasted Plum Tomato Sauce** (*p. 110*) *or* **other good tomato sauce**	250 ml
1 cup	beef stock	250 ml
	fresh Italian (flat-leaf) parsley, *chopped*	
	salt and freshly ground black pepper	

TIP:
• The sauce can be prepared ahead and refrigerated for a day or two, or frozen. Add parsley before serving.

• *Dried porcini mushrooms keep for months in the cupboard and have a rich, earthy flavour that enhances sauces and stews. This make-ahead sauce is delicious served over either pasta or polenta (p. 28), accompanied by a green salad and hot, crusty bread.*

1. Soak dried porcini mushrooms in warm water for 30 minutes.

2. Heat oil in a large heavy skillet over medium-high heat. Add sausage meat in chunks and brown on all sides, about 10 minutes.

3. Pour away any excess fat. Add tomato sauce, stock, and drained porcini mushrooms to the pan and simmer until sausage meat is cooked through.

4. Add parsley. Taste and adjust seasoning.

Serves 4.

VARIATION

• For a delicious change, serve the sauce on top of strands of crunchy spaghetti squash instead of pasta. Pierce the squash in several places and bake whole in a 375°F (190°C) oven until soft – about an hour. Cut in half, remove the seeds and, using a fork, gently separate and lift out the strands of flesh. Toss in a large bowl with a little olive oil, salt, pepper, parsley, and Parmesan cheese, and top with sauce. A 2–2½-lb (1 kg) spaghetti squash serves about 6. (Spaghetti squash is also good served at room temperature with a simple balsamic vinaigrette.)

Curried Vegetables & Couscous

2 tbsp	**olive oil**	30 ml
1	**large onion,** *chopped*	
2 cloves	**garlic,** *minced*	
1 tsp	**curry powder**	5 ml
1 tsp	**ground cumin**	5 ml
½ tsp	**ground coriander**	2 ml
½ tsp	**ground ginger**	2 ml
¼ tsp	**cayenne**	1 ml
2	**carrots,** *quartered lengthwise and chopped*	
½	**red pepper,** *seeded and chopped*	
1	**zucchini,** *halved and sliced*	
1	**yellow summer squash,** *halved and sliced*	
1 cup	**green beans,** *trimmed and cut in 2" (5 cm) lengths*	250 ml
1½ cups	**vegetable stock**	375 ml
½ cup	**couscous**	125 ml
	salt and freshly ground black pepper	

• *This fragrant and satisfying dish is open to many variations. You can use whatever vegetables you like – or have on hand – but be sure to chop them into appropriately sized chunks so that everything cooks in the same amount of time. (Harder vegetables should be cut smaller; delicate ones, larger.) Serve with warm pita bread or flatbread.*

1. Heat oil in a large, heavy frying pan or flameproof casserole. Add onion and garlic and cook over medium heat, stirring often, for about 5 minutes.

2. Stir in spices and vegetables, season lightly, and cook over medium heat for 2–3 minutes, stirring constantly until the vegetables are coated in the spicy onion mixture.

3. Add stock, bring to a boil, lower heat, cover, and simmer until vegetables are tender, about 10 minutes. Stir in couscous, cover, and cook for about 5 minutes longer. Adjust seasoning. Serve hot.

Serves 4.

TIPS:

• This dish is very good topped with some crumbled feta cheese and a sprinkling of chopped fresh coriander or parsley.

• Other vegetables that work well in this recipe include peas, mushrooms, eggplant, and cauliflower. Whatever combination you choose, you should have a total of 4 cups (1 L) of chopped vegetables.

• You could include boneless chicken pieces or cubed pork tenderloin, if you like. Brown meat lightly before you stir in the spices and vegetables.

CONTENTS

IN OTHER CHAPTERS...

Sides for Soup
The following recipes, which you'll find in other sections of the book, are delicious served alongside (or on top of) a bowl of soup:

QUICK TRICKS

Crispy Calzones (p. 125)

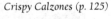

MEATLESS VARIATION

* These recipes (as well as all the soups) are meatless or have a meatless option

Eggplant & Basil Pesto Pizza (p. 131)

CROWD PLEASERS

Host a Pizza Potluck

You supply the pizza dough, a pot of homemade tomato sauce, and maybe a few bowls of grated or crumbled cheese. Ask each guest to bring along a favourite pizza topping. Put them all out on the table, and let everyone assemble his or her own personal pizza.

To help ensure you don't end up with a year's supply of pepperoni, here are some topping ideas to share:

- grilled vegetables: eggplant, zucchini, and peppers
- other vegetables: chopped tomato, red onion, mushrooms, olives, marinated or roasted artichoke hearts, cooked spinach
- meat and seafood: bacon, sausage, salami, slivered ham, tiny meatballs, prosciutto, slivers of grilled chicken, anchovies, shrimp, scallops, crabmeat, lobster

- cheeses to melt: mozzarella, fontina, Monterey Jack, provolone, Cheddar
- cheeses for flavour: feta, Asiago, Gorgonzola, goat cheese, Parmesan
- flavourings: garlic, herb, or hot pepper olive oil; herbs, fresh chilies or chili flakes, pesto, tapenade, salsa

Warning: The pile of toppings on the pizza shouldn't be so high that the heat can't penetrate the inner layers, or so wet that the crust becomes soggy. And hold the pineapple…

Assemble an Antipasto

An antipasto platter served with crusty bread makes a great light bite. Start with slices of grilled vegetables (p. 78) – eggplant, peppers, portobello mushrooms, zucchini. Add some grilled asparagus spears (p. 50) in a balsamic vinaigrette, thinly sliced prosciutto or Italian salami, bocconcini or mozzarella slices, and an assortment of olives. Garnish with shavings of Parmesan, strips of sun-dried tomatoes and fresh herbs. If you're feeling ambitious, add a bowl of Lemon Marinated Mussels (p. 20).

MORE SUMMER WEEKENDS

Carrot Ginger Soup

3 tbsp	**butter**	**45 ml**
1	**large onion,** *chopped*	
2 cloves	**garlic,** *minced*	
2 lbs	**carrots** *(about 8 large carrots), peeled and roughly chopped*	**1 kg**
2 tbsp	**fresh ginger,** *peeled and grated*	**30 ml**
1 tsp	**curry powder**	**5 ml**
6 cups	**chicken** *or* **vegetable stock**	**1.5 L**
	salt and freshly ground black pepper	
	fresh lemon *or* **lime juice** *(to taste)*	

TIPS:

• If you're using a ready-made stock, be sure to taste the soup before adding additional salt.

• The soup can be made ahead and stored in covered containers in the refrigerator for a day or two, or in the freezer for several weeks.

• *This simple puréed soup goes well with a Grilled Cheddar Sandwich or Melted Brie Baguette (facing page). Garnish it with chopped coriander or parsley and a dollop of yogurt or a handful of garlic croutons. It can also be served chilled.*

1. Heat butter in a large, heavy-bottomed saucepan. Add onions and garlic and cook over moderate heat, stirring occasionally, until they are soft and lightly golden – about 8–10 minutes.

2. Add carrots, grated ginger, and curry powder. Toss over heat for a few minutes.

3. Add stock and seasoning and bring to a boil. Lower heat, cover, and simmer until carrots are very tender, about 20 minutes.

4. Purée soup in batches in a blender or food processor.

5. Add lemon or lime juice and adjust seasoning to taste.

Serves 6.

Grilled Cheddar Sandwich
with Tomato Chutney

4	chunky slices of whole-wheat bread *or* challah	
	butter	
4	thin slices ham	
2 tbsp	tomato chutney	30 ml
¼ cup	Cheddar *or* Swiss cheese, *grated*	60 ml

QUICK TRICK:

Melted Brie & Roasted Red Pepper Baguette: Slice a baguette in half lengthwise and pull away some bread from the middle of each piece. Lightly brush each half with pesto or olive oil flavoured with fresh chopped basil. Place thinly sliced brie and roasted red pepper along the bottom piece. Cover with the top piece and press together firmly. Wrap tightly in foil. The sandwich can be made ahead to this point the night before.

When ready to eat, place the wrapped sandwich in a 350°F (180°C) oven and bake for about 15 minutes. Open the foil for the last 5 minutes to allow the bread to crisp a little. Cut into 8 pieces.

• *This is a sophisticated version of a childhood favourite. To ensure the sandwiches don't get mushy when grilled, make sure you start with bread that has good texture as well as flavour. The familiar white sliced won't do – the result will be a bland, soggy disappointment.*

1. Butter bread on both sides.

2. Place a slice of ham on two of the pieces of buttered bread. Spread each with half the chutney and sprinkle with half the grated cheese. Place another slice of ham on top and cover each with one of the remaining bread slices.

3. Heat a large, heavy frying pan over moderate heat. Place sandwiches in the pan, press down with a lifter, and cook for 2–3 minutes until the underside is golden. Turn sandwiches over, press down again, and continue to cook until cheese is melted and the other side is nicely browned. Serve hot with extra tomato chutney on the side.

Serves 2.

TIP:

• Cut the grilled sandwiches into small fingers or triangles and serve hot as snacks or appetizers.

Grilled Eggplant Soup
with Peppers & Tomatoes

3	red peppers	
1	large eggplant	
6	plum tomatoes	
3 tbsp	olive oil	45 ml
½	medium red onion, *chopped*	
3 cloves	garlic, *peeled and chopped*	
4 cups	chicken *or* vegetable stock	1 L
1 tsp	dried oregano	5 ml
	salt and freshly ground black pepper	
	sour cream, crème fraîche, *or* toasted croutons *(optional)*	

• *When dinner calls for veggies on the barbecue, grill extra eggplant, peppers, and tomatoes and set them aside to make a delicious smoke-flavoured soup the next day. Serve with Sweet Corn Muffins (p. 147), Devilish Cheese Twists (p. 17), or Herbed Buttermilk Biscuits (p. 133).*

1. Roast peppers on the barbecue over very high heat until skins are blistered and blackened on all sides, about 15 minutes. Set in a paper bag for 10 minutes to steam, then peel away charred skin, remove stem and seeds, and chop.

2. Cut eggplant in half and brush the cut sides lightly with oil. Lower heat to medium-high and grill, skin-side down, until skin is blackened and flesh is soft (about a half-hour over moderate heat). Remove skin and chop flesh.

3. Cut tomatoes in half lengthwise, lightly brush with oil, and set on grill, skin-side down. Grill about 10 minutes. Remove skin and seeds and chop.

4. Heat 2 tbsp (30 ml) oil in a large pot. Add onion, cook until lightly browned, then add garlic, eggplant, peppers, and tomatoes. Stir in stock, oregano, and seasoning, and simmer for about 30 minutes.

5. Purée soup in batches in a food processor or blender, or pass through a food mill until it is smooth. Taste and adjust seasoning. Top with sour cream, crème fraîche, or a few toasted croutons, and serve hot.

Serves 6.

Put on extra veggies when you're barbecuing dinner, then use them to make Grilled Eggplant Soup. Serve with Devilish Cheese Twists (p. 17).

Summer Minestrone

¼ cup	olive oil	60 ml
1	onion, *chopped*	
3 cloves	garlic, *chopped*	
2 stalks	celery, *thinly sliced*	
1	red pepper, *seeded and thinly sliced*	
1	dried hot pepper	
2	medium zucchini, *cut into chunks*	
1 can	plum tomatoes *(28 oz/796 ml)*	
1 can	white beans *rinsed and drained (19 oz/540 ml)*	
2 cups	stock *or* water	500 ml
1 tbsp	each fresh basil and thyme, *chopped* or	15 ml
1 tsp	each dried basil and thyme	5 ml
1	bay leaf	
½ lb	green beans, *trimmed and cut in pieces*	250 g
	Parmesan cheese, *grated*	

• *A flavourful combo of fresh summer vegetables topped with freshly grated Parmesan cheese. Accompany with crusty bread, Herbed Focaccia (facing page), or an Olive Baguette (Quick Trick, p. 133) for a great lunch or light dinner.*

1. Heat oil in a large, heavy pot. Add onion and cook over medium heat until soft.

2. Add garlic, celery, red pepper, and hot pepper, and cook for 5 minutes. Add zucchini and stir and cook for 2 minutes to coat the chunks in flavoured oil.

3. Chop tomatoes and add, along with their juice. Stir in white beans, stock or water, and herbs. Season to taste. Simmer, partially covered, for 20 minutes. Add green beans during last 10 minutes of cooking.

4. Remove hot pepper before serving. Adjust seasoning. Serve the soup hot with grated Parmesan cheese sprinkled on top.

Serves 6.

TIP:

• The minestrone has even richer flavour if left overnight, covered, in the refrigerator. It can also be frozen.

Herbed Focaccia

1 tbsp	dry active yeast	15 ml
½ cup	warm water	125 ml
3–3½ cups	unbleached hard wheat flour	750–875 ml
1 tsp	salt	5 ml
½ cup	cool water	125 ml
2 tbsp	olive oil	30 ml

olive oil *(for brushing tops of loaves and greasing pans)*

cornmeal *(for dusting pans)*

toppings *(sun-dried tomatoes, roasted peppers, halved cherry tomatoes, pitted olives, sliced grilled onions, grated Parmesan cheese)*

chopped fresh herbs *(rosemary, thyme, or basil)*

coarse salt

• *Focaccia is a crusty round or rectangular Italian flatbread baked with a variety of savoury toppings. It's great on its own as a snack, served with soups and salads, or split in half for sandwiches. This recipe comes from David Moore, the talented baker at All the Best Fine Foods.*

1. Dissolve yeast in warm water. Set aside for 10 minutes.

2. Combine flour and salt in a large bowl. Make a well in the centre and add the yeast mixture, cool water, and oil. Mix well with a wooden spoon, then turn out on a floured surface and knead for 8–9 minutes, until dough is smooth and no longer sticky. Place in a lightly oiled bowl, cover, and set aside in a warm place to rise until doubled in size (about 2 hours).

3. Punch down the dough. Roll out or stretch it into 1 large rectangle or 4–5 small circles about ¾" (2 cm) thick. Place on lightly greased baking sheets that have been dusted with cornmeal. Cover and allow to rise again, until doubled, about 1 hour.

4. Brush dough with olive oil and add your choice of toppings, pressing them into the dough. Sprinkle with herbs and coarse salt.

5. Place focaccia in a preheated 425°F (220°C) oven. Spray sides of oven with water from a spray bottle for 10 seconds (which helps create a crisp crust). Quickly close oven and bake for 25–30 minutes until bread is crisp and golden.

Makes 1 large loaf or 4–5 small ones.

Basic Pizza Dough

2¼–3 cups	all-purpose flour	560–750 ml
1 envelope	Fleischmann's Quick-Rise Instant Yeast *or* RapidRise Instant Yeast (*1 tbsp/15 ml*)	
1 tsp	salt	5 ml
1 tsp	sugar	5 ml
1 cup	water	250 ml
2 tbsp	olive oil	30 ml
	olive oil (*for greasing pans*)	
	cornmeal (*for dusting pans*)	

TIP:

• You can vary the flavour of the crust by replacing up to ½ cup (125 ml) of the regular flour with whole-wheat flour or cornmeal.

This recipe can turn you into a hero – especially when you're outside delivery range. Make a full-size pizza with all your favourite toppings (and try the ones on pp. 130 and 131), or create bite-sized versions for appetizers or snacks. (The kids will love you.) For speedy pizza "delivery," make the dough ahead, and then keep a batch in the freezer for emergencies. You can also use the dough to make calzones, the traditional Italian half-moon-shaped turnovers (facing page).

1. Toss 2 cups (500 ml) flour with yeast, salt, and sugar in a large bowl.

2. Heat water and oil until very warm (125°–130°F/50°–54°C, the equivalent of very hot, but not burning, tap water). Briskly stir or beat the liquid into the flour mixture for about 2 minutes.

3. Stir or knead in enough of the remaining flour to make a soft dough. Place on a lightly floured surface and knead until smooth and elastic, about 4 minutes. Shape dough into a smooth ball, and place in a well-oiled bowl, turning so the ball is coated with oil on all sides. Leave to rise, covered, in a warm, draft-free spot until doubled in size – about 30–60 minutes. (When a light, two-fingered poke makes a dent that stays, the dough is ready.)

4. Punch the dough down, and turn out onto a lightly floured surface. Divide dough according to what size pizzas you want to make. (See facing page.)

• Place 2½ cups (625 ml) flour in processor with yeast, salt, and sugar, and pulse to combine. Heat liquid ingredients (as in Step 2) and add through feed tube with motor running. If dough is too sticky, add 1–2 tbsp (15–30 ml) more flour. Dough should pull away from sides of bowl. Process for 30 seconds to knead, remove from bowl, knead briefly on floured surface, form into a ball, and proceed as with basic dough.

MAKE-AHEAD TIPS:

• To prepare pizza dough a day ahead: Let dough rise for about 30 minutes (Step 3), then place covered bowl in refrigerator overnight. Bring to room temperature before stretching the dough out.

• To freeze: Let the dough rise completely (through Step 3), then divide in two if you wish. Form each portion into a ball, wrap securely in a double layer of plastic wrap, and store in a freezer bag in the freezer for up to a month. Thaw overnight in the refrigerator, or 2–3 hours at room temperature.

5. Grease pizza pan(s) or baking sheet(s) and dust with cornmeal. Shape and stretch or roll the dough to fit. Cover with toppings and bake in a preheated 400°F (200°C) oven until the crust is lightly golden on the bottom and the toppings are hot – about 20 minutes for large pizzas, less for small.

Makes one 14" (35 cm) thick-crust pizza; two 12" (30 cm) thin-crust pizzas; four 8" (20 cm) individual pizzas; or twenty 3" (8 cm) bite-sized pizzas.

Crispy Calzones

Stuff these turnovers with the same ingredients you'd put on top of a pizza. Bite-sized ones make a popular party snack – try them filled with the toppings for Let's Go Greek Pizza (p. 130).

1. Divide the Basic Pizza Dough in half, then roll or stretch out each half as you would if you were making pizza. From each half, cut either two 8" (20 cm) circles, for calzones that each serve 1 as a substantial snack; or eight 4" (10 cm) circles, for mini party-size calzones.

2. On half of each circle, arrange layers of your favourite pizza toppings. Leave a ½" (1 cm) border around the edge of each circle.

3. Moisten the edge with water and fold the uncovered half of the dough over the filling. Pinch the edges securely closed. Prick the tops a couple of times with a fork to allow steam to escape. Brush the tops lightly with a mixture of egg yolk beaten with milk.

4. Place on lightly oiled baking sheets dusted with cornmeal and bake in a preheated 400°F (200°C) oven for 20 minutes until lightly golden.

Makes 4 large calzones or 16 bite-sized ones.

Red Lentil Soup
with Cumin & Lemon

2 cups	split red lentils	500 ml
8 cups	chicken *or* **vegetable stock**	2 L
1	**large tomato,** *peeled, seeded, and chopped*	
1	**onion,** *chopped*	
2 cloves	**garlic,** *chopped*	
1 tbsp	butter	15 ml
2 tsp	ground cumin	10 ml
	salt and freshly ground black pepper	
	lemon slices	
	sour cream, crème fraîche, *or* yogurt *(optional)*	
	fresh parsley, *chopped*	

TIP:

• Take care to read the cooking directions on the packages of lentils and beans you buy. Some brands have been processed to cook quickly; adjust the cooking time accordingly.

• *Lentils, peas, and dried beans are always useful basics to have on hand in the cupboard. This wonderfully fragrant soup uses red lentils – and is very easy to make. Crisped pita bread is a tasty accompaniment.*

1. Rinse lentils and discard any debris.

2. Bring stock to a boil in a large pot. Add lentils, tomato, onion, and garlic. Simmer, partially covered, until lentils are tender – about 45 minutes.

3. Purée soup in a food processor or food mill and press through a sieve if you prefer a very smooth texture. Return soup to the pot.

4. Melt butter in a small pan, add ground cumin, and stir over low heat for a couple of minutes. Stir the spice into the soup, heat through, and season with salt and lots of freshly ground pepper.

5. Top each serving with a lemon slice, chopped parsley, and a spoonful of sour cream, yogurt, or crème fraîche if you wish.

Serves 6.

Super Sandwich Combos

MORE SANDWICH IDEAS:
• Leftover sliced steak (p. 57) on a crusty bun with caramelized red onions (p. 12) and mayo with a hint of fresh tarragon or rosemary.

• Leftover grilled portobello mushrooms (p. 29) with garlic mayo, Swiss, and arugula on a focaccia that's been split and grilled.

• Leftover meatballs and sauce (p. 110) with roasted sweet and hot peppers on a toasted kaiser. Messy, but good.

QUICK TRICKS:
Add a dab of horseradish or wasabi (green Japanese horseradish) to Dijon mustard to give it some zip. (Try it on a sliced steak or pork sandwich.) Or make your own herb mustard: Add about 1 tbsp (15 ml) of fresh chopped herbs to 1/2 cup (125 ml) Dijon mustard. Tarragon mustard goes particularly well with cold sliced steak.

• Lemony Mayonnaise: To 1/2 cup (125 ml) mayo, add 1 tsp (5 ml) grated lemon zest and 1 tbsp (15 ml) fresh lemon juice. Add a little fresh chopped dill if you like.

• Let a main dish do double duty: Cook a little extra on the barbecue or stove the night before and use the leftovers for sandwiches the next day. Here are some tasty combos to try:

Pepper-Encrusted Loin of Pork Sandwich

Start with the Pepper-Encrusted Loin of Pork on p. 44. Stack thin slices on a crusty bun with sweet mustard; roasted red pepper slices or chili sauce; crisp greens such as arugula, romaine, or watercress; and mayo.

Cumin-Scented Lamb Wrap

Start with the grilled Cumin-Scented Leg of Lamb on p. 65. Spread tortillas with Red Pepper and Feta Spread (p. 32) or crumbled feta cheese. Add slices of cold grilled lamb and thin strips of grilled red and yellow peppers and zucchini, and roll up the tortillas.

Grilled Vegetables on Focaccia

Start with slices of Grilled or Pan-Roasted Vegetables (p. 78). Layer them on homemade (p. 123) or storebought focaccia that has been sliced in half horizontally and spread with pesto. Add sliced bocconcini or provolone.

Lemon Chicken Sandwich

Start with slices of Very Lemon Chicken (p. 99). Spread Lemony Mayonnaise (see Quick Trick, left) on a baguette. Add a layer of sliced chicken, crisp greens, and sliced roasted red and yellow peppers.

Easy Cantaloupe Soup

1	**large, ripe cantaloupe**
1 can	**frozen orange juice concentrate,** *thawed* *(12 oz/355 ml)*
	fresh mint leaves

TIP:

• This soup can also be made with honeydew melon, although the colour is not as vibrant.

It's hard to believe that a recipe with so few ingredients can taste so good. Serve this simple chilled soup as part of a light lunch on a summer day, along with an antipasto platter or a chicken salad and homemade biscuits (p. 133).

1. Remove rind and seeds from melon. Purée fruit in a food processor or blender or mash by hand until almost smooth.

2. Stir in juice concentrate (undiluted). Mix well. Cover and chill until serving.

3. Serve cold, garnished with fresh mint.

Serves 6.

Three ingredients and a couple of minutes – all that Easy Cantaloupe Soup requires.

Let's Go Greek Pizza

½ recipe Basic Pizza Dough (p. 124)		
1 tbsp	olive oil	15 ml
½	medium red onion, *finely chopped*	
1 clove	garlic, *finely chopped*	
½ cup	spinach, *cooked, squeezed dry, and chopped*	125 ml
½ cup	mozzarella cheese, *grated*	125 ml
¼ cup	pitted black olives, *sliced*	60 ml
½ cup	feta cheese, *crumbled*	125 ml
drizzle	flavoured olive oil	
1 tbsp	fresh parsley, *chopped (optional)*	15 ml
	salt and freshly ground black pepper	

TIP:

• To make a flavoured olive oil for this pizza, put a clove of sliced garlic, a twist of lemon peel, and some chopped fresh or dried rosemary into ¼ cup (60 ml) of extra-virgin olive oil. Allow to stand for at least 15 minutes before using.

• *A delicious change from the familiar pizza with tomato sauce. And if you prepare the dough and the spinach topping ahead – see p. 125 and the tip below – you can have hot, crispy pizza on the table in 30 minutes or less.*

1. Heat olive oil in a heavy frying pan, add onion, and cook over medium heat until soft. Add garlic and cooked spinach, season lightly, and continue to cook over medium heat for 3–4 minutes.

2. On a lightly floured surface, stretch or roll the dough to form a 12" (30 cm) circle, or cut into ten 3" (8 cm) rounds. Place on oiled baking sheets that have been dusted with cornmeal.

3. Cover dough with about half the mozzarella. Sprinkle on the spinach mixture, the remaining mozzarella, the olives, and the crumbled feta. Drizzle flavoured olive oil on top.

4. Bake in a preheated 400°F (200°C) oven for about 20 minutes, until the crust is lightly golden on the bottom and the topping is very hot. Sprinkle with chopped parsley if desired and serve immediately.

Serves 2 as a main course, or 4–6 for snacks.

TIP:

• You can make the spinach topping (Step #1) a day or two ahead; keep refrigerated until needed.

Eggplant & Basil Pesto Pizza

½ recipe	**Basic Pizza Dough (p. 124)**	
2 tbsp	**basil pesto**	30 ml
1	**medium eggplant,** *thinly sliced and grilled or roasted*	
½	**roasted red pepper,** *chopped (optional)*	
drizzle	**garlic-flavoured olive oil** *(optional)*	
¼ cup	**goat cheese or feta cheese**	60 ml
	fresh parsley, *chopped (optional)*	
	salt and freshly ground black pepper	

• *This pizza is a real crowd pleaser – particularly when made on 3" (8 cm) rounds for bite-sized versions.*

1. On a lightly floured surface, stretch or roll the dough to form two 8" (20 cm) circles, or cut into ten 3" (8 cm) rounds. Place on oiled baking sheets that have been dusted with cornmeal.

2. Spread a light even layer of basil pesto on the dough, and top with a layer of eggplant and red pepper, if using. (Chop the eggplant into smaller pieces if you are making 3"/8 cm pizzas.) Season with salt and pepper and a little garlic-flavoured olive oil if you like.

3. Bake in a preheated 400°F (200°C) oven for 15 minutes. Remove from oven and add a topping of crumbled goat cheese or feta cheese. Return to oven to bake for about 5 minutes longer, until the crust is lightly golden on the bottom. Sprinkle with chopped parsley if desired and serve immediately.

Serves 2 as a main course, or 4–6 for snacks.

TIP:

• To make a pizza on the barbecue, partially prebake the dough base for about 10 minutes in a 400°F (200°C) oven. Cool, wrap well, and refrigerate or freeze until needed. When ready to use, return crust to room temperature, add toppings, and place on a preheated grill. Close the lid and bake, over indirect heat (see p. 9), for about 10 minutes, until base is crisp and nicely browned and toppings are hot.

Spicy Stuffed Enchiladas

2 tbsp	vegetable oil	30 ml
1	medium onion, *chopped*	
1	red pepper, *seeded and chopped*	
2	zucchini, *halved lengthwise and sliced*	
1½ cups	corn kernels *(fresh or frozen)*	375 ml
2 tbsp	jalapeño peppers *(fresh or canned), diced*	30 ml
2 tbsp	fresh coriander *or* parsley, *chopped*	30 ml
½ cup	Monterey Jack cheese *or* mild Cheddar, *grated*	125 ml
8	corn *or* flour tortillas *(8"/20 cm)*	
2 cups	mild tomato salsa *or* tomato sauce	500 ml
½ cup	sour cream	125 ml
dash	salt	

• *A spicy vegetable filling is wrapped in either corn (yellow) or flour (white) tortillas and baked with tomato sauce or salsa. Serve with sour cream on top and diced fresh tomato, finely shredded lettuce, and red onion alongside.*

1. Heat oil in a large frying pan over moderate heat. Add onion and cook until soft and lightly browned, about 10 minutes. Add red pepper, zucchini, corn, and salt and cook for about 5 minutes longer.

2. Remove pan from heat and stir in jalapeño peppers, coriander or parsley, and cheese.

3. If you're using corn tortillas, soften them by frying in hot oil for a few seconds on each side (you'll need about ½ cup/125 ml of oil in a large frying pan), then drain on paper towel. Flour tortillas don't require softening.

4. Place about ⅓ cup (75 ml) of the vegetable filling along the bottom third of each tortilla and roll up neatly.

5. Spread a thin layer of tomato sauce or salsa in the bottom of a 9" x 13" (23 cm x 33 cm) baking dish and arrange the filled tortillas on top, side by side. Drizzle the remaining sauce over the top.

6. Bake in a 375°F (190°C) oven for about 20 minutes or until heated through. Serve hot, topped with sour cream.

Serves 4.

Herbed Buttermilk Biscuits

2 cups	all-purpose flour	500 ml
1 tsp	baking powder	5 ml
½ tsp	baking soda	2 ml
1 tsp	dried thyme	5 ml
½ tsp	salt	2 ml
6 tbsp	cold butter	90 ml
¾–1 cup	buttermilk	175–250 ml

(see Pantry, p. 155)

TIP:

• To make formed biscuits, turn dough out onto a floured board. Pat with floured fingers to make an even layer about ¾" (2 cm) thick and cut with a floured biscuit cutter or glass. Brush tops with egg wash or cream if you like, and bake as above.

• *Try these quick biscuits hot from the oven with soup, with eggs at breakfast, or as a topping for Fresh Vegetable Stew (p. 109).*

1. Combine flour, baking powder, baking soda, dried thyme, and salt in a large bowl or food processor.

2. Cut in butter until mixture resembles coarse crumbs. (Use a knife and your fingertips; or pulse briefly, then turn into a bowl.)

3. Add buttermilk and toss lightly with a fork to make a soft dough.

4. Drop mixture by spoonfuls onto greased baking sheets or on top of stew in a shallow baking dish. Bake in preheated 425° F (220°C) oven until biscuits are lightly browned, 12–15 minutes. Serve hot with butter.

Makes 16 biscuits (2"/5 cm).

QUICK TRICK:

An Olive Baguette makes a welcome change from plain garlic bread: Cut a baguette on the diagonal into 8 slices, not quite all the way through. Brush each slice with a little garlic-flavoured olive oil, then spread with tapenade (a purée of black olives that's available ready-made, or you can make your own – see p. 16). Re-form the baguette, lightly brush the outside with oil, and wrap in foil. Place in a 400°F (200°C) oven for about 10 minutes. Open foil and heat bread for a few more minutes until the top is crispy. Serve hot.

CONTENTS

QUICK TRICKS

IN OTHER CHAPTERS...

Coffee Cakes

*You'll find the following cakes –
a treat for breakfast or brunch – in
Section VII (Sweet Stuff):*

Fruit Toppings and Sauces

*You'll find the following fruit toppings
and sauces – great on pancakes,
waffles, and yogurt – in Section VII
(Sweet Stuff):*

5 Easy Ways to Elevate Breakfast above the Ordinary

1. *Real maple syrup: For the pancakes and French toast*

2. *Homemade-style preserves: The type that drips off your toast and tastes like pure fruit – and pure summer*

3. *Butter: Health concerns notwithstanding, nothing compares in flavour for cooking your eggs or melting on toast*

4. *Great breads, muffins, and buns: Homemade – or homemade style*

5. *Real coffee: Freshly ground, freshly brewed*

CROWD PLEASERS

Brunch for a Bunch

The first three brunches will serve 12 (and can be scaled down for fewer), with most of the work done ahead. (The stratas and French toast are assembled the night before and then just put in the oven in the morning.) To make life even easier, have several thermal jugs on hand, so you can keep the supply of freshly brewed hot stuff coming. And appoint a sous-chef, who can watch the bacon, toast the muffins, and help you get everything from oven to table.

Brunch for a Bunch No. 1

Melon Medley *(p.149)*
   (make double the recipe)

Asparagus Prosciutto Strata and Asparagus Pepper Strata *(p.136)*
   (or double the recipe of one strata, if meat isn't an issue)

Toasted English muffins

Blueberry Brunch Cake *(p.168)*

A No-Cook Brunch for a Bunch

Breakfast Trifle *(p.141)*
   (make double the recipe)

Basket of warm bran muffins *(p.148)* **and toasted bagels**

Fruit preserves

Breakfast cheese plate *(fontina, Gouda, cream cheese, havarti, Swiss)*

Thinly sliced ham

Pear Crumble Cake *(p.178)*

Brunch for a Bunch No. 2

Fresh orange & pineapple wedges or slices

Overnight French Toast with Blueberries *(p.150)*
   (make double the recipe)

Maple Syrup or Blueberry Maple Syrup *(p.153)*

Grilled bacon or sausage

Brunch for a Smaller Bunch
(serves 4, or double the recipes to serve 8)

Fresh fruit juice or orange and grapefruit segments

Diner-Style Sausage Hash *(p.146)*

Poached *(p.138)* **or fried eggs**

Sweet Corn Muffins *(p.147)* **or brown toast**

Can't-Resist Chelsea Buns *(p.143)*

Asparagus Prosciutto Strata

1 loaf	**French bread,** *cut in ½" (1 cm) slices on the diagonal*	
1 cup	**milk**	250 ml
1 lb	**asparagus,** *trimmed*	500 g
¼ lb	**prosciutto,** *chopped*	125 g
1 cup	**Swiss** *or* **provolone cheese,** *grated*	250 ml
¼ cup	**Parmesan cheese,** *grated*	60 ml
4	**eggs**	
¼ tsp	**nutmeg,** *freshly grated*	1 ml
¼ cup	**35% cream**	60 ml
	salt and freshly ground black pepper	

VARIATION:

• For a vegetarian option, replace the prosciutto with slivers of roasted red and/or yellow peppers.

• *Puffed and golden brown – like a soufflé without the finickiness – a strata is a savoury baked custard that looks wonderful on the table and is a great dish for a special breakfast or brunch. Do the work the night before and pop the strata in the oven the next morning. Accompany it with a roasted pepper salad or a simple tossed green one.*

1. The night before serving, dip bread slices in milk and gently press out as much liquid as possible. Arrange a layer of bread slices in the bottom of a buttered ovenproof dish approximately 8" x 8" (20 cm x 20 cm).

2. Blanch the asparagus in boiling water for 5 minutes. Cut in 1" (2 cm) pieces.

3. Spread the asparagus pieces evenly over the bread slices and sprinkle with prosciutto and two-thirds of the Swiss (or provolone) and Parmesan cheese. Then add another layer of bread and top with the remaining cheese.

4. Beat eggs together with nutmeg, salt, and pepper, and pour over the strata. Cover with plastic wrap and leave overnight in the refrigerator.

5. The following day, bring strata to room temperature. Pour the cream over top. Bake at 350°F (180°C) until puffed and lightly browned, about 40–50 minutes. Serve hot.

Serves 6.

Breakfast Pizza

½ recipe	**Basic Pizza Dough** *(p. 124)*	
1	**sausage (sweet** *or* **hot Italian)**	
4 slices	**lean side bacon, peameal bacon,** *or* **ham**	
2 tbsp	**tomato sauce**	**30 ml**
½ cup	**mozzarella cheese,** *grated*	**125 ml**
1	**egg**	
	fresh parsley, *chopped (optional)*	

TIP:

• The sausage and bacon can be cooked a day ahead and refrigerated.

• *Try this twist on the bacon-and-eggs theme for a hearty breakfast or brunch.*

1. Remove casing from sausage. Break up sausage meat in a frying pan set over moderate heat, and cook until no longer pink, about 5 minutes. Remove and set aside.

2. Cut ham or bacon slices in half. Grill or lightly fry until half cooked. Drain on paper towel and set aside.

3. On a lightly floured surface, stretch or roll the dough to form one 10"–12" (25–30 cm) circle. Place on an oiled baking sheet or pizza pan that has been dusted with cornmeal.

4. Spread a light, even layer of tomato sauce over the dough, add about half the mozzarella, then the crumbled sausage, ham or bacon slices, and the rest of the cheese. Make a small hollow in the cheese in the centre of the pizza and break an egg into it.

5. Bake in a preheated 400°F (200°C) oven for 15 minutes. Remove from oven and carefully break open the egg yolk with a fork, pulling the yolk gently through the cheese topping towards the edge of the pizza. Continue baking for about 5 minutes longer until the crust is lightly golden on the bottom and the topping is piping hot. Serve hot, sprinkled with chopped parsley if you like.

Serves 2.

Poached Eggs with Spinach
& Quick Hollandaise Sauce

1 tbsp	**butter**	15 ml
1	**small onion,** *finely chopped*	
½ cup	**35% cream**	125 ml
2 cups	**fresh** *or* **frozen spinach,** *cooked and drained*	500 ml
pinch	**nutmeg,** *freshly grated*	
pinch	**cayenne**	
¼ cup	**Parmesan cheese,** *freshly grated*	60 ml
4–8	**poached eggs** *(Quick Trick, below)*	
4	**English muffins,** *toasted*	
1–2 cups	**Quick** **Hollandaise** *or* **Virtuous Hollandaise** *(next page)*	250–500 ml
	salt and freshly **ground black pepper**	

TIPS:

• Prepare the spinach mixture the night before, cover and refrigerate, and warm before serving.

• The spinach mixture also makes a delicious omelette filling.

• *A sublime combination when you're in the mood for something special. It's an easy dish to make – although an extra pair of hands helps ensure everything is ready at the right moment when you're serving a number of people.*

1. Heat butter in a medium-sized frying pan, add onion, and cook until soft. Add cream and a dash of salt and pepper, and simmer until cream is reduced by half, 3–5 minutes. Stir in cooked spinach, nutmeg, cayenne, and Parmesan cheese, and adjust seasoning.

2. Serve spinach mixture on toasted English muffins, with poached eggs and Quick Hollandaise or Virtuous Hollandaise sauce on top.

Serves 4.

QUICK TRICK:

For perfect poached eggs, fill a frying pan, preferably non-stick, with water to a depth of about 2" (5 cm). Add 1 tsp (5 ml) white vinegar and ¼ tsp (1 ml) salt. (This helps to keep the eggs together.) Bring water to a boil, then lower heat to a gentle simmer. One at a time, crack each egg into a small bowl and slide the egg into the simmering water. Simmer for about 2 minutes for a soft egg. Remove with a slotted spoon and drain.

If you are poaching eggs for a crowd, slide the cooked eggs into a bowl of ice water. Slip them back into simmering water for a minute to reheat at serving time.

Poached Eggs with Spinach and Hollandaise, with bacon on the side. If you're worried about being too decadent, you can opt for the Virtuous Hollandaise (p. 140).

Two Hollandaise Sauces

Quick Hollandaise

4	large egg yolks	
3 tbsp	lemon juice	45 ml
1 tbsp	water	15 ml
pinch	salt	
pinch	cayenne	
1 cup	unsalted butter, *melted*	250 ml

Virtuous Hollandaise

1½ cups	light mayonnaise	375 ml
½ cup	sour cream	125 ml
2 tsp	lemon juice	10 ml
1 tsp	Dijon mustard	5 ml
pinch	cayenne	
	salt and freshly ground black pepper	

Quick Hollandaise

A classic Hollandaise sauce uses raw eggs. The method here, put forward by the American Egg Board, heats the egg yolks to kill any lurking salmonella bacteria, first diluting the yolks with a healthy amount of lemon juice and a dash of water to prevent hardening.

1. Combine the egg yolks, lemon juice, and water in a small, preferably non-stick, frying pan and stir constantly over very low heat just until the mixture bubbles at the edge and becomes creamy, about 1 minute. Immediately lift from the heat, stir constantly while mixture cools, then scrape into a blender or food processor. Blend briefly and season with salt and cayenne.

2. With motor running, pour in warm melted butter in a slow steady stream. The sauce will thicken as the butter is added. Taste and adjust seasoning. If necessary, keep the sauce warm for a short period in a bowl over hot water.

Makes about 1½ cups (375 ml).

Virtuous Hollandaise

If the butter- and egg-yolk-laden Hollandaise is too rich for your blood, try this one. If you want a really virtuous version, use light sour cream too.

1. Combine ingredients thoroughly. Taste and adjust seasoning.

Makes 2 cups (500 ml).

Baked Eggs in Tomatoes

4	just-ripe firm tomatoes	
	salt and freshly ground black pepper	
1 clove	garlic, *minced*	
4	eggs	
3 tbsp	35% cream	45 ml
1 tbsp	tomato paste	15 ml
½ tsp	dried oregano	2 ml
½ tsp	dried basil	2 ml
2 tbsp	Parmesan cheese, *grated*	30 ml

QUICK TRICK:

Breakfast Trifle is a delicious way to start the day, and a feast for the eyes, too. For 6–8 people, you'll need 3 cups (750 ml) granola, 4 cups (1 L) 1% French vanilla yogurt, 2 sliced bananas, 3 oranges cut into sections, and 1 pint (500 ml) sliced strawberries. Starting at the bottom of a large glass bowl, layer half the granola, half the yogurt, the bananas, oranges, and strawberries, and the remainder of the yogurt. Top with remaining granola. Garnish with whole berries if desired.

• *Eggs and sun-ripened field tomatoes are just made for each other. This is a perfect dish for August mornings, when flavourful tomatoes are easy to come by. Serve with peameal bacon and hot, buttered Sweet Corn Muffins (p. 147).*

1. Slice stem ends from tomatoes, scoop out seeds and pulp, sprinkle with salt and pepper, and set upside down for a few minutes to drain juices.

2. Place tomatoes in a buttered ovenproof dish; make it a tight fit so they don't tip over. Sprinkle a little garlic in each tomato shell and break an egg on top.

3. Combine cream, tomato paste, and herbs and spoon a little over each egg. Sprinkle with Parmesan cheese.

4. Bake in a 350°F (180°C) oven for about 20 minutes or until eggs are set. Serve immediately.

Serves 4.

Can't-Resist Chelsea Buns

Caramel Topping

½ cup	brown sugar	125 ml
3 tbsp	corn syrup	45 ml
¼ cup	butter	60 ml
¼ cup	pecan halves, *toasted*	60 ml
4 tsp	dried cherries	20 ml

Spicy Nut Filling

zest of	½ orange, *chopped*	
zest of	½ lemon, *chopped*	
3 tbsp	pecans, *toasted and finely chopped*	45 ml
¼ cup	brown sugar	60 ml
¼ cup	sultanas	60 ml
¼ tsp	nutmeg	1 ml
½ tsp	cinnamon	2 ml

Dough ingredients on next page

● *For the past few years, I have worked beside David Moore, a very talented bread baker. This is his version of the Chelsea Bun – which people line up for every weekend at the All the Best bake shop. You don't have to get up too early in the morning to wow your family and friends with this treat: You can prepare the buns before you go to bed, then bake them fresh in the morning.*

1. To make the Caramel Topping, place sugar, corn syrup, and butter in a small saucepan. Set over medium heat and stir while sugar melts. Raise heat and allow mixture to bubble for 4–5 minutes. Pour into a 7" (18 cm) round cake pan and sprinkle pecans and dried cherries on top. Set aside.

2. To make the Spicy Nut Filling, toss all ingredients together in a small bowl. Set aside.

3. To make the dough, place warm water and 1 tsp (5 ml) sugar in a bowl. Sprinkle yeast on top and let stand for 5 minutes until foamy.

4. Stir in warm milk, egg, the remaining sugar, half the flour, and the salt. Add ¼ cup (60 ml) of the butter and stir to combine.

5. Beat in remaining flour, then knead (or beat with the dough hook on your mixer) until dough is smooth, soft and elastic, 5–8 minutes.

6. Place the dough in a clean bowl and cover with plastic wrap. Set aside in a warm, draft-free spot for an hour, or leave it, covered, in the refrigerator overnight to rise slowly.

Please turn to next page

Make them the night before, bake them in the morning, then set these irresistible Chelsea buns on the breakfast table and wait for the compliments.

Can't-Resist Chelsea Buns, continued

Dough

2 tsp	active dry yeast	10 ml
1/4 cup	warm water	60 ml
3 tbsp	sugar	45 ml
1/3 cup	warm milk	80 ml
1	egg	
2 cups	flour	500 ml
3/4 tsp	salt	3 ml
1/4 cup +2 tbsp	soft butter	60 ml + 30 ml

TIP:

• For a different taste, substitute walnuts and cranberries for the pecans and cherries in the topping.

7. When ready to bake the buns, punch the dough down and bring to room temperature. On a lightly floured surface roll out dough to form a rectangle about 12" x 6" (30 cm x 15 cm), approximately 1/2" (1 cm) thick. Brush surface with remaining soft butter and sprinkle Nut Filling evenly on top. Roll dough up tightly lengthwise, like a jelly roll, and cut into 6 equal pieces.

8. Arrange the pieces, cut side down in the prepared pan. Cover with plastic wrap and set aside in a warm spot for dough to rise for about an hour.

9. Bake in a preheated 350°F (180°C) oven for 25–30 minutes.

10. Remove pan from oven and set on a rack for a minute. Set the rack over parchment paper or a baking sheet to catch any hot dripping caramel. Flip the pan over and then carefully lift it off. Allow Chelsea Buns to cool before serving.

Makes 1 loaf or 6 irresistible portions.

TIPS:

• You can prepare the buns through Step 8 the night before – except instead of putting them in a warm place to rise, put them in the refrigerator to rise slowly overnight. In the morning, bring the buns to room temperature – this will take at least an hour – before baking.

• When you have rolled up the dough like a jelly roll, you can wrap it well and freeze it for 2–3 weeks. When ready to serve, thaw the roll, slice into 6 pieces, and proceed as from Step 8 above.

• You can substitute a sweet or enriched dough made in your bread machine for this dough.

Fried Fresh Fish with Salsa

1½ lbs	fresh fish fillets	750 g
1 cup	buttermilk *(see Pantry, p. 155)*	250 ml
1 cup	fine cornmeal	250 ml
3 tbsp	butter	45 ml
	Roasted Tomato Corn Salsa *(p. 20)* *or* other salsa	
	salt and freshly ground black pepper	

TIP:

• You can substitute sour milk for buttermilk: Put 1 tbsp (15 ml) of lemon juice or vinegar in a measuring cup. Add milk to make 1 cup. Let stand 5 minutes; stir well.

• *A great way to showcase the catch at breakfast. Although some people swear by crushed potato chips or pulverized Ritz crackers for the coating, I like plain cornmeal: It provides the requisite crunchiness and tastes great with salsa on the side. Roasted Tomato Corn Salsa (p. 20) goes well, or use a favourite prepared salsa to save time.*

1. Season fish fillets lightly. Dip them first in buttermilk, then in lightly seasoned cornmeal to coat evenly.

2. Heat butter in a large heavy frying pan over medium heat. Fry fish until lightly browned on one side, about 5 minutes. Turn and cook the other side a minute or two more, depending on the type of fish. Generally, it is done when the flesh separates into moist flakes when tested.

3. Serve the fillets straight from the pan with salsa on the side.

Serves 4.

Diner-Style Sausage Hash

3 cups	cooked potatoes	750 ml
	(baked or boiled), peeled and cut into small cubes	
¾–1 lb	sausages	375–500 g
1	medium onion, *finely chopped*	
1 tbsp	parsley, *chopped*	15 ml
1 tbsp	oil	15 ml
2 tbsp	butter	30 ml
	salt and freshly ground black pepper	

TIPS:

• Bake or boil a few extra potatoes when you're making supper to get a quick start on next morning's breakfast or brunch.

• The hash mixture can be prepared the night before (through Step #2) and stored, covered, in the refrigerator.

• Add a chopped stalk of celery, half a chopped pepper (red and/or green), or a few lightly browned, sliced mushrooms to the hash if you like.

• *Crispy browned potatoes, just like the diner makes, are the perfect match for eggs. This twist on classic hash uses your favourite sausage instead of corned beef. Serve hot with fried or poached eggs on top (for perfect poached eggs, see Quick Trick, p. 138), or scrambled eggs on the side, and brown toast.*

1. Prick sausages and simmer in enough water to cover for 5 minutes. Remove from water and allow to cool, then pull away the casing and roughly chop the filling.

2. Toss crumbled sausage with potatoes, onion, parsley, and salt and pepper to taste.

3. Heat oil and butter in a non-stick frying pan. Add sausage mixture and press down with a spatula to make an even layer. Cook, covered, over moderate heat for about 10 minutes to heat through.

4. Remove lid, raise heat, and cook 5 minutes longer until nicely browned on the bottom. Flip the hash out onto a plate. Add a little more butter to the pan and when it's hot, slide the hash back in, unbrowned side down. Cook for a few more minutes until the underside is golden. Serve in hot wedges straight from the pan with eggs alongside or on top.

Serves 4.

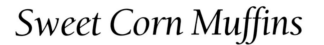

Sweet Corn Muffins

1 cup	flour	250 ml
1 cup	cornmeal	250 ml
2 tsp	baking powder	10 ml
½ tsp	salt	2 ml
¼ cup	sugar	60 ml
1	**egg,** *beaten*	
1 cup	milk	250 ml
dash	hot sauce	
¼ cup	**butter** *or* **shortening,** *melted*	60 ml
1 cup	**cooked corn kernels** *(approx. 1 ear of corn)*	250 ml

• *These muffins go well with eggs and are a great way to use up that leftover ear of corn from dinner.*

1. Preheat oven to 425°F (220°C). Grease muffin cups or line them with muffin papers.

2. Combine flour, cornmeal, baking powder, salt, and sugar in a bowl.

3. Combine egg, milk, and hot sauce, and lightly blend into dry ingredients. Don't overmix. Stir in melted butter or shortening and corn.

4. Spoon into muffin cups, filling about ¾ full. Bake in preheated oven for 15–20 minutes or until a toothpick inserted in muffin comes out clean.

Makes 12 muffins.

TIPS:

• Corn cooked on the barbecue adds a wonderful roasted flavour to these muffins.

• You can substitute frozen corn (defrost before adding) or even canned if fresh isn't available.

The Ultimate Bran Muffin

1²/₃ cups	natural bran	400 ml
¾ cup	all-purpose flour	175 ml
1 tsp	baking soda	5 ml
½ tsp	salt	2 ml
¼ tsp	baking powder	1 ml
1	egg	
¾ cup	brown sugar, *packed*	175 ml
¼ cup	oil *or* **melted butter**	60 ml
1 cup	buttermilk (*see Pantry, p. 155*)	250 ml
2 tbsp	molasses	30 ml
¾ cup	raisins	175 ml

• *This recipe, the creation of professional baker Jill Snider, produces the best bran muffins I know. They're full of bran flavour – but, unlike some bran muffins, very moist and light. And the batter will keep for up to a week in the fridge.*

1. Preheat oven to 375°F (190°C). Grease muffin cups or line them with muffin papers.

2. Combine bran, flour, baking soda, salt, and baking powder. Set aside.

3. In large bowl, combine egg, brown sugar, oil or butter, buttermilk, molasses, and raisins. Mix well.

4. Add dry ingredients, stirring until moistened.

5. Fill muffin cups ¾ full. Bake for 20–25 minutes, or until top springs back when lightly touched.

Makes 12 muffins.

TIP:

• **Replace raisins with your favourite dried or fresh fruit. Try chopped dates or dried apricots, dried cranberries, fresh blueberries, grated apple, or chunks of nectarine.**

Carrot Apple Muffins

3 cups	all-purpose white flour *or* half each whole wheat and white	750 ml
1 tsp	baking soda	5 ml
2 tsp	baking powder	10 ml
1 tsp	cinnamon	5 ml
½ tsp	salt	2 ml
1½ cups	sugar	375 ml
1¼ cups	sunflower oil	300 ml
4	large eggs	
2½ cups	carrots (*about 5–6 carrots*), *grated*	625 ml
2 cups	apples (*about 2 apples*), *peeled and chopped*	500 ml
1 tsp	fresh orange rind, *grated*	5 ml

TIP:

• Golden Delicious apples are indeed delicious in this recipe.

• *Even when the larder is just about empty, you're likely to find a few carrots and apples around for these moist, fruity muffins. They can be made ahead – the recipe makes a big batch – stored in the freezer, and warmed for a quick breakfast.*

1. Preheat oven to 375°F (190°C). Grease muffin cups or line them with muffin papers.

2. Combine flour, baking soda, baking powder, cinnamon, and salt. Set aside.

3. In a separate bowl, beat sugar, oil, and eggs until light and fluffy.

4. Blend dry mixture into beaten egg mixture. Fold in carrots, apples, and orange rind.

5. Spoon batter into muffin cups, filling about ¾ full. Bake for 25–35 minutes, or until a toothpick inserted in the centre comes out clean.

Makes about 2-dozen medium-sized muffins.

QUICK TRICK:

Put together a Melon Medley to accompany a basket of fresh-from-the-oven muffins: Slice half a honeydew and half a cantaloupe into thin wedges and remove skin. Arrange melon slices on a platter. In the middle, pile fresh strawberries that have been tossed with a little sugar (if desired) and fresh chopped mint. Serves 4.

TIP: Select melons that feel heavy for their size and have a pronounced aroma.

Overnight French Toast
with Blueberries

1 cup	brown sugar, *packed*	250 ml
1¼ tsp	cinnamon	6 ml
¼ cup	butter, *melted*	60 ml
12 slices	bread	
1½ cups	fresh blueberries	375 ml
5	eggs	
1½ cups	milk	375 ml
1 tsp	vanilla	5 ml
½ tsp	salt	2 ml

TIPS:

• You can substitute raspberries, peaches, or apples for the blueberries.

• Try raisin or egg bread or brioche instead of plain white.

• *This blueberry-filled breakfast and brunch dish is a lazy cook's dream: You can prepare it entirely ahead the night before and then just slip it in the oven in the morning. Serve warm with maple syrup and grilled bacon or sausage alongside.*

1. Combine brown sugar, cinnamon, and melted butter. Mix well. Sprinkle ⅓ of mixture evenly in bottom of a 9" x 13" (23 cm x 33 cm) pan.

2. Cover with 6 slices of bread. Sprinkle another ⅓ of sugar mixture over bread and scatter berries on top.

3. Place remaining bread on fruit. Sprinkle with remaining sugar mixture.

4. Beat eggs, milk, vanilla, and salt together. Pour evenly over bread. Press down lightly. Cover with plastic wrap and refrigerate overnight, or let stand at room temperature for 2 hours.

5. Bake, uncovered, at 350°F (180°C) for 40–45 minutes, or until puffed and golden.

Serves 6.

QUICK TRICK:

Start the day with a Fruit Smoothie: Combine ¾ cup (175 ml) orange juice, 1 cup (250 ml) sliced strawberries, and 2 sliced bananas and whirl in a blender with 2 crushed ice cubes until smooth. (If you prepare the fruit ahead and freeze it, you can eliminate the ice.) For a different taste, substitute ½ cup (125 ml) cranberry juice and ½ cup plain yogurt for the orange juice. Serves 2.

Overnight French Toast with Blueberries can be prepared the night before. Then it just needs to be baked before serving in the morning.

Banana Buttermilk Pancakes

1 cup	**very ripe bananas** *(about 2 large bananas), mashed*	250 ml
2 tsp	**lemon juice**	10 ml
1 cup	**buttermilk** *(see Pantry, p. 155)*	250 ml
1	**egg**	
1 tsp	**vanilla**	5 ml
1 tsp	**lemon rind,** *grated*	5 ml
3 tbsp	**butter,** *melted and cooled*	45 ml
1 cup	**all-purpose flour** *(or part all-purpose and part buckwheat or whole wheat)*	250 ml
2 tbsp	**sugar**	30 ml
2 tsp	**baking powder**	10 ml
½ tsp	**baking soda**	2 ml
½ tsp	**salt**	2 ml

TIP:

•The batter can be prepared the night before and kept, covered, in the refrigerator.

• *A delicious way to use up those overripe bananas in the fruit bowl. Serve these light, fluffy cakes with Blueberry Maple Syrup (facing page) or plain maple syrup poured over top and sliced bananas or strawberries alongside.*

1. Blend mashed bananas and lemon juice.

2. Combine banana mixture with buttermilk, egg, vanilla, lemon rind, and melted butter in a large bowl.

3. In a separate bowl, combine dry ingredients. Stir dry ingredients into banana/buttermilk mixture, taking care not to overmix.

4. Brush surface of a large non-stick frying pan with butter. When the pan is hot, spoon in the batter using a ¼ cup (60 ml) measure or a small ladle. Cook for 2–3 minutes over medium-high heat. When the surface is smooth and small bubbles appear, turn pancake over once only and cook briefly to brown the other side.

Makes a dozen 4" (10 cm) pancakes.

QUICK TRICK:

Super Scrambled Eggs with Smoked Salmon: Beat 8 eggs with ¼ cup (60 ml) milk or cream. Cook gently until eggs are almost set – heat toughens the protein in eggs, so cook over low heat to keep them creamy – then stir in 2 tbsp (30 ml) deli-style cream cheese and 1 tbsp (15 ml) chopped fresh chives or green onion tops. Serve topped with strips of smoked salmon (or blanched asparagus, or slices of roasted red and yellow pepper). Add Sweet Corn Muffins (p. 147), toasted bagels, or whole-wheat toast to complete the breakfast.

Blueberry Corn Griddle Cakes

½ cup	cornmeal	125 ml
½ tsp	salt	2 ml
1 tbsp	maple syrup	15 ml
½ cup	boiling water	125 ml
½ cup	all-purpose flour	125 ml
2 tsp	baking powder	10 ml
1	egg	
3 tbsp	butter, *melted and cooled*	45 ml
½ cup	milk	125 ml
1 cup	blueberries	250 ml
1 tsp	lemon zest, *grated*	5 ml

TIP:

• Have a pot of melted butter and a pastry brush on the stove so you can quickly grease the pan between batches of pancakes.

• *Every cook should have a pancake recipe in his or her repertoire for those times when there's no boxed mix on hand. Besides, from-scratch batter gives you a chance to do something a little different. The cornmeal gives these cakes a pleasing crunch, and the blueberries make them taste like summer. Serve a sky-high pile in a pool of Blueberry Maple Syrup (Quick Trick, below).*

1. In a large bowl, combine cornmeal with salt, maple syrup, and boiling water. Stir and set aside.

2. Combine flour and baking powder. In a small bowl, combine egg, melted butter, and milk.

3. Mix dry ingredients alternately with liquid ingredients into cornmeal mixture, stirring lightly until smooth. Fold in blueberries and lemon zest. Don't overmix.

4. Spoon the batter onto a hot, lightly buttered griddle or frying pan, using a small ladle or ¼ cup (60 ml) measure. Cook until small bubbles appear on the top of each pancake, then turn to brown the other side.

5. Serve hot on warm plates with warm Blueberry Maple Syrup.

QUICK TRICK:

Blueberry Maple Syrup: Combine in a small saucepan ¼ cup (60 ml) water, 2 strips lemon zest, 1 cup (250 ml) blueberries, and ½ cup (125 ml) maple syrup. Bring gently to a simmer, cover, and cook 5 minutes. Serve warm or at room temperature. The syrup will keep 3–5 days in the refrigerator.

Chocolate Nests and Crunchy Peanut Butter Shells (p. 167) and Strawberry Yogurt Popsicles (p. 160)

CONTENTS

QUICK TRICKS

Ginger Shortbread (p. 161) with Strawberry Rhubarb Compote (p. 162)

BARBECUE FRIENDLY

* These recipes use the barbecue, or have an option for barbecue cooking

Top 3 for Chocolate Fanatics

1. *Decadent Fudge Cookies: Three types of chocolate in each fudgy bite (p. 174)*

2. *Espresso Ice Cream Loaf: Rich chocolate ice cream on the bottom, vanilla ice cream with chocolate crunch in the middle, and chocolate sauce on top (p. 163)*

3. *Couldn't-Be-Easier Chocolate Banana Cake: Dark, moist, and chocolatey. If you want to go over the top, add chocolate frosting and/or ice cream (p. 156)*

STOCKING THE SWEET PANTRY

Beyond the basics – all-purpose flour, baking powder, baking soda, cornstarch, white and brown sugar, icing sugar, honey, corn syrup, old-fashioned and quick-cook oats, cocoa, vanilla – here are a few other supplies to have on hand that will help you whip up delicious desserts and other baked treats:

• **Dried fruit:** Not just dates and raisins. Dried cranberries, cherries, and blueberries are now readily available in packages and in bulk-food stores. They last almost forever and can be used to add intense fruit flavour to cookies, cakes, and salads. Unsweetened coconut and crystallized ginger (if you like it) are good additions, too.

• **Chocolate:** Unsweetened, semi-sweet, milk chocolate, and white chocolate. Squares, chunks, and chips. Great for snacking as well as baking. For the ultimate indulgence, use the finest quality imported chocolate – my favourite is Callebaut.

• **Nuts:** Pecans, walnuts, peanuts, hazelnuts, sliced or slivered almonds. Toasting the nuts helps bring out their flavour: Put in a shallow baking pan in a 375°F (190°C) oven for 3–6 minutes, stirring often, so they become evenly and lightly browned.

• **Buttermilk powder:** Available in bulk-food stores, buttermilk powder is a great staple to have on hand. If a recipe calls for 1 cup (250 ml) buttermilk, put $\frac{1}{4}$ cup (60 ml) of the powder in a 1 cup (250 ml) measure, fill with cold water, and mix well. If you are baking or making pancakes, add the powder to the dry ingredients and the water to the liquid ones. (Buttermilk powder meant specifically for baking is sold in cans in some U.S. supermarkets.)

• **Graham crackers or crumbs:** Great for a quick crust.

• **Instant espresso powder:** Adds a real shot of coffee flavour, and intensifies the taste of chocolate.

• **A little spice is nice:** The most frequently used spices for baking are cinnamon, ginger, and cloves; buy a fresh supply each spring for the best flavour. Cardamom is a favourite of mine – especially with apples. A whole nutmeg keeps for ages and makes a huge difference in taste compared with the previously ground stuff. Try it freshly grated in a fruit smoothie.

Couldn't-Be-Easier
Chocolate Banana Cake

2 cups	sugar	500 ml
1¾ cups	all-purpose flour	425 ml
¾ cup	cocoa	175 ml
1½ tsp	baking powder	7 ml
1½ tsp	baking soda	7 ml
1 tsp	salt	5 ml
2	eggs	
1 cup	ripe banana (2 large bananas), mashed	250 ml
1 cup	warm water	250 ml
½ cup	milk	125 ml
½ cup	oil	125 ml
1 tsp	vanilla	5 ml

• *This cake is dark and chocolatey, and so moist it doesn't require any frosting – although it sure is delicious served with vanilla ice cream, crème fraîche, or custard on top. It can be whipped up in minutes, and is a great way to use up a couple of overripe bananas.*

1. Preheat oven to 350°F (180°C). Grease a 9" x 13" (23 cm x 33 cm) pan.

2. Combine sugar, flour, cocoa, baking powder, baking soda, and salt. Mix well.

3. In a large bowl, whisk together eggs, banana, warm water, milk, oil, and vanilla until blended.

4. Add dry ingredients, whisking until smooth and thoroughly blended. Batter will be thin.

5. Pour into prepared pan. Bake for 35–40 minutes, or until toothpick inserted in centre comes out clean.

6. Cool cake in pan on wire rack.

Makes about 16 servings.

Lynda's No-Bake Bars

2½ cups	quick-cook oats	625 ml
6 tbsp	cocoa	90 ml
1 cup	unsweetened coconut	250 ml
1 cup	sliced *or* slivered almonds, *toasted*	250 ml
1 cup	dried cherries *or* cranberries *(optional)*	250 ml
½ cup	butter	125 ml
½ cup	milk	125 ml
1½ cups	sugar	375 ml
1 tsp	vanilla	5 ml

• *You don't even have to turn on the oven for this treat, which takes less than 10 minutes to put together. It comes from one of the great cooks at All the Best Fine Foods, who developed the recipe based on one from her grandmother.*

1. Combine oats, cocoa, coconut, almonds and dried fruit (if using) in a large bowl.

2. Place butter, milk, and sugar in a saucepan and bring to a boil, stirring to combine. Remove from heat and stir in vanilla.

3. Pour mixture over dry ingredients and mix well. Scrape into a lightly greased 8" x 8" (20 cm x 20 cm) or 9" x 9" (23 cm x 23 cm) pan.

4. Refrigerate for about half an hour to allow bars to harden, then cut into squares. (You don't need to keep them refrigerated.)

Makes about 20 squares.

Strawberry Meringue Cake

¾ cup	all-purpose flour	175 ml
¼ cup	cornstarch	60 ml
1½ tsp	baking powder	7 ml
½ cup	soft butter	125 ml
1½ cups	sugar	375 ml
4	eggs, *separated*	
2 tsp	vanilla	10 ml
2 tbsp	milk	30 ml
½ cup	sliced almonds, *toasted*	125 ml

Filling and decoration

1 cup	whipping cream	250 ml
½ tsp	vanilla	2 ml
1 tbsp	icing sugar	15 ml
1 qt	fresh strawberries	1 L

• *This take on the classic strawberry shortcake features crunchy meringue layers with lashings of whipped cream and juicy berries in between. It looks impressive, but is easy to make. You can bake the meringue layers a couple of days ahead, then assemble the cake shortly before serving.*

1. Preheat oven to 350°F (180°C). Lightly butter and flour two 9" (23 cm) round cake pans.

2. Sift together flour, cornstarch, and baking powder, and set aside.

3. Beat butter until light. Add ½ cup (125 ml) sugar and continue beating until mixture is light and fluffy. Beat in egg yolks, one at a time. Add 1 tsp (5 ml) vanilla.

4. Blend in dry ingredients and milk. Spread batter in prepared cake pans.

5. Let egg whites reach room temperature, then beat until soft peaks form. Gradually beat in the remaining sugar and vanilla. Spread a layer of meringue on top of each layer of batter and sprinkle with almonds.

6. Bake in preheated oven about 25 minutes, or until a toothpick inserted in the centre of the cake comes out clean and the top is an even light brown. Set aside to cool in the pans.

Please turn to next page

The almond-covered meringue on each layer gives a delectable crunch to this take on traditional strawberry shortcake.

Strawberry Meringue Cake, continued

QUICK TRICK:
For the kids, make Strawberry Yogurt Popsicles (shown in photo, pp. 164–165). Crush 2 cups (500 ml) hulled strawberries in a food processor or with a potato masher. Stir in 1½ cups (375 ml) plain yogurt and 2 tbsp (30 ml) icing sugar. Process or mix until smoothly blended. Divide the mixture evenly into 10 small paper drink cups (the 3 oz/100 ml size). Cover each with foil. Make a small slit in centre of foil and insert a wooden stick or plastic spoon handle through the foil and into each cup. (Or use plastic Popsicle-style moulds.) Freeze until firm, at least 3 hours. To serve, tear away the paper cup. Makes 10.

To assemble the cake:

1. Whip cream, vanilla, and icing sugar together until soft peaks hold their shape.

2. Trim and halve the berries, saving the nicest ones to decorate the top of the cake.

3. Remove cake layers from pans and place one on a platter meringue-side down. Spread with a layer of whipped cream and a layer of berries.

4. Top with the other cake layer meringue-side up. Decorate top with berries and swirls of whipped cream. Serve any remaining berries alongside.

Makes 8 slices.

Ginger Shortbread

2 cups	all-purpose flour	500 ml
1 cup	dark brown sugar	250 ml
2 tbsp	ground ginger	30 ml
1 tsp	baking soda	5 ml
pinch	salt	
1 cup	butter, *softened*	250 ml
2 tbsp	crystallized ginger, *finely chopped (optional)*	30 ml

VARIATION:

• Add 1 oz (30 g) finely grated unsweetened dark chocolate to half the mixture. Bake as above.

QUICK TRICK:

Low-fat yogurt – 1% M.F. or 2% M.F. – can be turned into a wonderful substitute for high-fat whipped cream: Set the yogurt, with a pinch of salt added, to drain in a sieve lined with a double layer of cheesecloth or a paper coffee filter. Refrigerate. After about 30 minutes, the yogurt will have the consistency of light whipped cream. Stir in a little honey and serve as a dessert topping.

• *A crisp, spicy, buttery cookie that's fabulous with fruit, especially summer berries, rhubarb, and peaches. Pile the fruit on the cookie, and add a topping of lightly sweetened whipped cream or yogurt (see Quick Trick, below). Try the shortbread with Strawberry Rhubarb Compote (p. 162), Mixed Berry Sauce (p. 180), or Ginger Spiced Pears (p. 162) for an irresistible dessert.*

1. Preheat oven to 325°F (170°C). Lightly butter and flour two 9" (23 cm) round cake pans.

2. In a large bowl toss together the flour, sugar, ginger, soda, and salt. Blend in butter with your fingers or a pastry blender, until mixture forms fine crumbs. Add crystallized ginger (if using).

3. Press mixture into the two prepared pans to form a smooth, even layer. Prick surface all over lightly with a fork.

4. Bake in preheated oven for 40–45 minutes until edges are lightly browned. Let cool in the pan for 5 minutes, then cut into narrow wedges and cool on racks. Store in an airtight container.

Make 32 wedges.

Mix & Match Fruit Toppings

Strawberry Rhubarb Compote

½ cup	sugar	125 ml
¼ cup	orange juice	60 ml
1 strip	orange peel, *(orange part only, no pith)*	
2 cups	rhubarb, *chopped*	500 ml
2 cups	strawberries, *sliced*	500 ml

Ginger Spiced Pears

½ cup	sugar	125 ml
1 cup	water	250 ml
1	cinnamon stick *(3"/7.5 cm)*	
2 strips	lemon zest	
3 slices	fresh ginger, *(¼" /5 mm thick)*	
6	almost-ripe pears, *peeled, cored, and quartered*	

Strawberry Rhubarb Compote

• *Serve over Ginger Shortbread (previous page) or pound cake (p. 175) and top with whipped cream or yogurt. Also try it on pancakes at breakfast.*

1. Combine sugar, orange juice, and orange peel in a saucepan over moderate heat. Stir until sugar dissolves, then add rhubarb and simmer, covered, until tender (about 20 minutes).

2. Fold in strawberries and simmer for about 5 minutes. Set aside to cool, then refrigerate until serving. *Makes 4 servings.*

Ginger Spiced Pears

Serve alongside Pear Crumble Cake (p. 178) or on top of Ginger Shortbread (previous page). You can use the same method with plums, peaches, or apples.

1. Combine sugar, water, cinnamon, lemon zest, and ginger in a medium-sized saucepan over moderate heat. Stir while sugar dissolves, then simmer the syrup for 5 minutes.

2. Add pears to the syrup, cover the pot, and simmer for about 5 minutes more, or until pears are just tender. (Cooking time will vary depending on the variety of pear and the ripeness of the fruit.)

3. Set aside and chill. Remove whole spices before serving. *Makes 6 servings.*

(The Strawberry Rhubarb Compote is shown in the photo on the previous page.)

Espresso Ice Cream Loaf

2 cups	chocolate ice cream, *slightly softened*	500 ml
3 cups	vanilla ice cream, *slightly softened*	750 ml
1½ tsp	instant espresso powder	7 ml
2–3	Skor chocolate bars, *crushed (39 g each)*	
¼ cup	toasted almonds, *chopped (optional)*	60 ml
	chocolate sauce *(optional)*	

• *A make-ahead dessert that looks as fabulous as it tastes.*

1. Line an 8½" x 4½" (1.5 L) loaf pan with plastic wrap, leaving the ends hanging over the sides of the pan. Spread chocolate ice cream evenly in pan. Place in freezer while making the top layer.

2. Mix vanilla ice cream and espresso powder until blended. Stir in 2 chocolate bars and nuts (if using). Spread over chocolate ice cream. Bring edges of plastic wrap over the top to seal tightly and freeze in the loaf pan until firm, at least 8 hours.

3. To serve, unmould onto cutting board, Remove plastic wrap. Cut into slices. If desired, drizzle slices with chocolate sauce or an additional crushed Skor bar.

Makes about 12 servings.

 QUICK TRICK:
Lift economy-style ice cream to gourmet heights with these easy additions. Slightly soften the ice cream, then fold in the goodies and refreeze until serving time.

• crushed peanut brittle in vanilla or butterscotch-ripple ice cream

• chopped almond bark (dark, milk, or white chocolate) in any flavour ice cream

• crushed striped mint candies in vanilla ice cream

• crushed candy bars (Skor, Crispy Crunch, etc.) in any flavour ice cream

• chopped cookies in any flavour ice cream

• 1–2 tbsp (15–30 ml) instant espresso powder in 1 L vanilla or chocolate ice cream

Overleaf, clockwise from left: Espresso Ice Cream Loaf (this page), Peachy Thick Shake (p. 183), Caramel Almond Ice Cream Sandwiches (p. 166), Strawberry Yogurt Popsicles (p. 160), and ice cream in Chocolate Nests and Crunchy Peanut Butter Shells (p. 167).

Caramel Almond
Ice Cream Sandwiches

40	soda crackers, plain *or* five-grain, salted *or* unsalted	
1 cup	butter	250 ml
1 cup	brown sugar, *packed*	250 ml
1 cup	sliced almonds	250 ml
	ice cream	

TIPS:

• For a more elegant presentation, cut the squares into triangles or fingers and serve them alongside a dish of ice cream.

• Graham crackers can also be used in this recipe. You'll need about 32 squares.

• *The squares are so yummy they may not make it to the sandwich stage.*

1. Preheat oven to 375°F (190°C). Generously grease a 10" x 15" (25 cm x 38 cm) jelly-roll pan or baking sheet with sides.

2. Line the pan with a single layer of crackers, trimming to fit if necessary.

3. Melt butter in a medium-sized saucepan. Add sugar. Cook over medium heat, stirring constantly, until mixture is thoroughly blended, 3–4 minutes. (Do not allow it to boil.)

4. Stir in almonds. Carefully spread mixture over crackers.

5. Bake in preheated oven for 7–8 minutes, or until golden. Cool about 30 minutes. Cut into squares while still warm.

6. Sandwich 2 squares together with a generous helping of ice cream in the middle, about 1" (2.5 cm) thick. Press firmly together. Slip each sandwich into a plastic bag or wrap tightly in plastic wrap. Freeze.

Makes about 15 sandwiches.

(Caramel Almond Ice Cream Sandwiches are shown in the photo on the previous page.)

Chocolate Nests
& Crunchy Peanut Butter Shells

Chocolate Nests

1 cup	chocolate chips	250 ml
½ cup	corn syrup	125 ml
½ cup	peanut butter	125 ml
4 cups	crisp rice cereal	1 L

Crunchy Peanut Butter Shells

1 cup	brown sugar, *packed*	250 ml
1 cup	corn syrup	250 ml
1 cup	peanut butter	250 ml
7 cups	corn flake cereal, *slightly crushed*	1.75 L
1¼ cups	peanuts, *chopped*	300 ml

• *These crispy shells make edible bowls for your favourite ice cream – a change from plain old cones that will delight kids and adults alike.*

Chocolate Nests

1. Heat chips and syrup in large saucepan until chips are melted. Add peanut butter, heat, and stir until smooth. Add cereal. Mix well.

2. Scoop mixture into greased, large muffin cups until they're about ¾ full. Press a large indentation in the centre of each to form a shell. Chill in refrigerator until firm.

Makes about 15 shells.

Crunchy Peanut Butter Shells

1. Heat sugar and syrup in a large saucepan to dissolve. Add peanut butter and heat, stirring until smooth.

2. Combine cereal and nuts in a large bowl. Add syrup mixture. Mix well. Cool slightly.

3. Scoop mixture into greased, large muffin cups until they're about ¾ full. Press a large indentation into the centre of each to form a shell. Chill in refrigerator until firm.

Makes about 18 shells.

(Chocolate Nests and Crunchy Peanut Butter Shells are shown in the photo on pp. 164–165.)

Blueberry Brunch Cake

Base

½ cup	butter, *softened*	125 ml
⅔ cup	sugar	150 ml
1	egg	
2 tsp	lemon rind, *grated*	10 ml
1½ cups	all-purpose flour	375 ml
2 tbsp	poppy seeds	30 ml
½ tsp	baking soda	2 ml
¼ tsp	salt	1 ml
½ cup	sour cream	125 ml

Filling

2 cups	fresh blueberries	500 ml
⅓ cup	sugar	75 ml
2 tsp	all-purpose flour	10 ml
¼ tsp	nutmeg	1 ml

Glaze (optional)

⅓ cup	icing sugar, *sifted*	75 ml
1–2 tsp	milk	5–10 ml

● *This attractive, easy-to-make cake is great for brunch or dessert. It brings out the fresh flavour of blueberries to the fullest.*

1. Preheat oven to 350°F (180°C). Grease and flour the bottom and sides of a 9" (23 cm) springform pan.

2. Beat butter and sugar until light and fluffy. Add egg and lemon rind. Beat 2 minutes more at medium speed.

3. Combine flour, poppy seeds, baking soda, and salt. Stir into butter mixture, alternately with sour cream. Spread dough evenly over bottom and 1" (2.5 cm) up sides of pan. Base and sides should be about ¼" (6 mm) thick.

4. Thoroughly toss together all ingredients for filling. Spoon over base.

5. Bake in preheated oven for 40–50 minutes, or until crust is golden. Cool slightly; carefully remove the springform side of the pan.

6. To finish, combine the icing sugar and just enough milk to make a syrupy consistency. Drizzle over top of cake.

Makes 10–12 servings.

TIP:
● The glaze on top is optional – you can use a quick, light dusting of icing sugar to complete the cake instead.

Blueberry Brunch Cake showcases one of the favourite berries of summer. It's not overly sweet either, especially if you just dust the top with icing sugar.

Nutty Ice Cream Crumbles

• These crumble toppings are wonderful sprinkled on ice cream, either plain or drizzled with sundae sauce. Store leftovers in tightly sealed containers.

Crumble No. 1

¾ cup	sugar	175 ml
6 tbsp	butter, *melted*	90 ml
1½ cups	unblanched almonds *or* pecans, *coarsely chopped*	375 ml

1. Blend sugar and butter. Stir in nuts. Spread on jelly-roll pan or baking sheet with sides.

2. Bake in 375°F (190°C) oven for 12–18 minutes, stirring every 5 minutes, until golden-brown. If necessary, drain off excess butter. Cool completely.

3. Put in a plastic bag and crush to make coarse crumbs.

Crumble No. 2

½ cup	butter	125 ml
1 cup	rolled oats	250 ml
1 cup	hazelnuts, *coarsely chopped*	250 ml
½ cup	brown sugar, *packed*	125 ml

1. Melt butter in large frying pan. Stir in remaining ingredients.

2. Cook, stirring constantly over medium heat for 8–10 minutes, or until mixture is golden-brown. Cool completely.

3. Put in a plastic bag and crush to make coarse crumbs.

Each Crumble makes about 3 cups (750 ml).

QUICK TRICK:
Chocolate Crackle Sundae Sauce: Just like the soda-fountain favourite, this warm sauce hardens on cold ice cream. Chop 4 squares of semisweet or white chocolate (4 oz/120 g) and melt with ¼ cup (60 ml) butter on low heat or in a microwave until smooth. Spoon warm sauce on ice cream and leave for a few minutes to harden.

Creamy Coffee Tortoni

4 cups	vanilla ice cream, *slightly softened*	1 L
1 tbsp	instant espresso powder	15 ml
½ cup	amaretti (Italian-style macaroons), *crushed*	125 ml
¼ cup	toasted almonds, *chopped*	60 ml

Topping

3 tbsp	amaretti, *crushed*	45 ml
2 tbsp	toasted almonds, *chopped*	30 ml

QUICK TRICK: Serve cappuccino and dessert in the same cup, with a Coffee Ice Cream Float: Fill a mug ⅔ full of black coffee and sweeten to taste. Add a scoop of vanilla ice cream, and stir slightly. Add another scoop of ice cream, sprinkle with grated chocolate or cinnamon, and serve immediately – with a spoon and a straw.

• *Individual treats with the kick of coffee and the crunch of nuts and macaroons.*

1. Mix ice cream and espresso powder until well blended. Stir in amaretti and nuts.

2. Line muffin cups with a double layer of muffin papers. Spoon in ice cream to almost fill cups.

3. Combine amaretti and almonds for topping. Sprinkle over ice cream mixture.

4. Cover tins with plastic wrap and freeze until firm, at least 3 hours. Remove from freezer 5 minutes before serving.

5. Serve in the paper cups for easy entertaining, or remove and place on dessert plates.

Makes about 12 servings.

Giant Oatmeal Cookies
with Cranberries & Pecans

¾ cup	butter	175 ml
1 cup	brown sugar, *packed*	250 ml
¼ cup	honey	60 ml
1	egg	
1 tsp	vanilla	5 ml
	zest of 1 orange, *finely grated*	
¾ cup	all-purpose flour	175 ml
½ tsp	salt	2 ml
½ tsp	baking soda	2 ml
3 cups	old-fashioned large-flake oats	750 ml
1½ cups	dried cranberries	375 ml
1 cup	pecans, *chopped*	250 ml

TIP:

• Use a heaped tablespoon of batter to make medium-sized cookies. Reduce baking time to 10–12 minutes.

• *Make the batter ahead and store it in covered containers – it will keep in the refrigerator for a few days – then have fresh-baked cookies when the urge strikes.*

1. Preheat oven to 350°F (180°C). Lightly grease 2 baking sheets or line them with parchment.

2. Cream butter, sugar, and honey together in a large bowl at medium speed with an electric mixer. Add egg, vanilla, and orange zest, and continue to beat until light and creamy.

3. In a separate bowl, combine flour, salt, and baking soda, and stir into the creamed mixture.

4. Add oats, cranberries, and pecans, and stir until well mixed.

5. Drop batter by ¼ cup (60 ml) measures onto prepared baking sheets. Wet your hands with water and use your palms to flatten the cookies, so they are about ⅜" (7 mm) thick. Bake for 14–16 minutes until lightly browned at the edges but still soft in the centres. Remove with a lifter to wire racks to cool.

Makes 2-dozen large cookies.

VARIATION:

• For Chocolate Chip Oatmeal Cookies, omit the orange zest and cranberries. Add 1 tsp (5 ml) cinnamon and 1½ cups (375 ml) chocolate chips. Bake as above.

Giant Oatmeal Cookies with Cranberries & Pecans and Decadent Fudge Cookies (p. 174): Guaranteed not to make it to the cookie jar.

Decadent Fudge Cookies

14 oz	**semi-sweet chocolate,** *cut in chunks (about 2 full cups/500 ml)*	400 g
2 oz	**unsweetened chocolate,** *cut in chunks (about 1/3 cup/75 ml)*	50 g
1/4 cup	**unsalted butter**	60 ml
3	**large eggs,** *lightly beaten*	
1/2 cup	**white sugar**	125 ml
1 1/2 cups	**brown sugar**	375 ml
1 tsp	**vanilla**	5 ml
1/2 cup	**all-purpose flour**	125 ml
1/2 tsp	**baking soda**	2 ml
pinch	**salt**	
1/2 cup	**pecans,** *toasted and chopped*	125 ml
1 cup	**semi-sweet chocolate chips**	250 ml
1/2 cup	**dried cherries,** *softened in water and patted dry (optional)*	125 ml

• *If you want to keep these triple-chocolate cookies from disappearing in the blink of an eye, you'll need to store them in a locked tin under your bed! They're great for making ice cream sandwiches, by the way.*

1. Preheat oven to 375°F (190°C). Grease and flour baking sheets or line them with parchment.

2. Melt semi-sweet chocolate, unsweetened chocolate, and butter in a bowl set over simmering water.

3. Beat eggs, white and brown sugar, and vanilla until light and fluffy.

4. In a separate bowl, toss together the flour, baking soda, salt, pecans, and chocolate chips; set aside.

5. Pour egg/sugar mixture into melted chocolate and combine thoroughly. Stir in dry ingredients. Set aside for a few minutes until mixture cools and batter is firm enough to scoop.

6. Drop by teaspoonfuls onto prepared baking sheets. Bake for about 6 minutes – just until the top begins to crack and the inside is still fudgy.

7. Cool on the baking sheets for 10 minutes, then transfer to racks. When completely cool, store in an airtight tin.

Makes 3-dozen cookies.

(The triple-chocolate Decadent Fudge Cookies are shown in the photo on the previous page.)

Versatile Pound Cake

2 cups	all-purpose flour	500 ml
2 tsp	baking powder	10 ml
¼ tsp	salt	1 ml
½ cup	butter, *softened*	125 ml
1 cup	sugar	250 ml
3	eggs, *lightly beaten*	
1 tsp	vanilla	5 ml
1 tsp	lemon *or* orange zest, *grated*	5 ml
1 cup	sour cream	250 ml

QUICK TRICK:

Dress up a plain pound cake with a lemon or orange glaze: In a small pan, combine the juice of 1 lemon or orange and ¼ cup (60 ml) sugar. Heat just to melt sugar. Pour syrup over warm cake.

● *This recipe is a lifesaver, as it can help you create a number of quick desserts. Top it with fresh berries or Mixed Berry Sauce (p. 180) – and a dollop of whipped cream or ice cream. Layer it with custard and fruit to make a summer trifle. Turn it into a Pear (or Apple or Plum) Crumble Cake (p. 178). Dip it in egg and grill it for a French-toast-like dessert (p. 176). Or drizzle it with a lemon or orange glaze (see Quick Trick, below) and serve it on its own.*

1. Preheat oven to 350°F (180°C). Lightly grease (or line with parchment) an 8" x 8" (2 L) square pan or a 9" x 5" (2 L) loaf pan.

2. Combine flour, baking powder, and salt. Set aside.

3. Cream butter and sugar until light and fluffy. Add eggs, one at a time. Stir in vanilla and lemon or orange zest.

4. Fold in flour mixture alternately with sour cream.

5. Spoon batter into prepared pan. Bake on the middle rack of the oven for about an hour, or until a wooden skewer poked into the centre of the cake comes out clean. (Test cake after 50 minutes.) Cool in pan on a wire rack for 10 minutes, then remove from pan and cool completely.

Makes 12–16 slices.

Grilled Pound Cake
with Warmed Strawberries

2 cups	strawberries, *halved or quartered*	500 ml
¼ cup	sugar	60 ml
4 slices	pound cake (³⁄₄"/2 cm thick)	
1	**egg,** *lightly beaten*	
2 tbsp	milk	30 ml
2 tbsp	orange liqueur (*such as Cointreau or Grand Marnier*)	30 ml
	whipped cream (*optional*)	

QUICK TRICK:

When you have the barbecue going, Rum-Glazed Fruit makes a wonderful dessert: Remove skin and eyes from a ripe pineapple. Cut into ½" (1 cm) slices and remove core. Or peel peaches, cut in half, and remove stones. Combine ¼ cup (60 ml) each of dark rum, unsalted butter, and brown sugar in a small saucepan over low heat until butter is melted and sugar dissolved. Add 2 tbsp (30 ml) fresh orange or lime juice. Brush mixture on fruit and grill over medium heat about 5 minutes a side. Serve hot with ice cream.

• *This recipe turns French toast into a dessert prepared on the barbecue – an appealing idea if you're eating outdoors on a warm night. The Versatile Pound Cake (previous page) is great for this recipe, or take a shortcut and use a store-bought cake.*

1. Combine berries and sugar in an aluminum pie plate. Let stand at room temperature to allow juices to form. Stir occasionally.

2. Preheat grill on high for a few minutes.

3. Place pie plate with strawberry mixture on one side of grill to warm. Stir occasionally.

4. Beat egg, milk, and liqueur in a small shallow dish. Dip each slice of cake into egg mixture, turning to coat both sides thoroughly. Using egg lifter, place each slice on grill. Turn after 3 or 4 minutes, or when nicely browned, and brown second side.

5. Place each slice of cake on a dessert plate and spoon berries on top. Garnish, if desired, with whipped cream. Serve immediately.

Serves 4.

TIPS:

• Add in other berries, such as raspberries or blueberries.

• Replace the orange liqueur with orange juice plus ¼ tsp (1 ml) vanilla extract.

Strawberries and cream on top of pound cake treated like French toast – who could resist?

Pear Crumble Cake

Cake

	batter for Versatile Pound Cake *(p.175)*	
3	**ripe pears,** *peeled, cored, and cut into thick slices*	

Ginger Crumble Topping

½ cup	**brown sugar**	**125 ml**
⅓ cup	**flour**	**75 ml**
1 tsp	**ground ginger**	**5 ml**
1 tbsp	**crystallized ginger,** *diced (optional)*	**15 ml**
¼ cup	**cold butter,** *cut in small chunks*	**60 ml**

TIPS:

• The cake can be baked ahead and frozen (best when used within a couple of weeks).

• Substitute sliced apples or plums for the pears.

• Purée chilled Ginger Spiced Pears (p. 162) in a food processor or blender with a little of their syrup and serve the cake on a pool of the purée.

• *Delicious warm for breakfast. To dress it up for dessert, serve it with Ginger Spiced Pears (p. 162) or Ginger Spiced Pear Purée (Tip, below) on the side.*

1. Make Crumble Topping: In a large bowl, combine sugar, flour, and ginger(s). Cut in cold butter until mixture resembles coarse crumbs. (Or combine in a food processor using on/off pulses.) Set aside.

2. Preheat oven to 350°F (180°C). Lightly grease, or line with parchment, a 9" (23 cm) springform pan or a 9" x 9" (23 cm x 23 cm) baking pan.

3. Spoon pound cake batter into prepared pan. Arrange sliced pears on top and cover evenly with Ginger Crumble Topping.

4. Bake on the middle rack of the preheated oven for about an hour, or until a wooden skewer poked into the centre of the cake comes out clean. (Test cake after 50 minutes.) Cool in pan on a wire rack for 10 minutes, then remove from pan and cool completely, right side up. Serve warm or at room temperature.

Makes 12–16 slices.

Sweet & Simple Peach Tart

Sweet Crust

2½ cups	all-purpose flour	625 ml
⅔ cup	sugar	175 ml
½ tsp	salt	2 ml
1 cup	soft butter, *cut in pieces*	250 ml
2	egg yolks	
1 tsp	vanilla	5 ml
1 tbsp	lemon juice	15 ml

Tart

6–8	ripe peaches, *peeled and sliced*	
1 tsp	cinnamon	5 ml
5 tbsp	sugar	75 ml
1	egg, *beaten*	
1 cup	sour cream	250 ml

VARIATION:
• Replace the peaches with thinly sliced nectarines, plums, or apples.

• *A crisp, sweet crust layered with fruit of the season. The topping is just a small, decadent extra. Great for serving a crowd, since it makes a nice, big pan.*

1. Prehat oven to 400°F (200°C). Butter a 10" x 15" (25 cm x 38 cm) jelly-roll pan or baking sheet with sides.

2. Combine dry ingredients for crust in a large bowl or in the bowl of a food processor. Quickly blend or pulse in butter.

3. Mix egg yolks, vanilla, and lemon juice in a small bowl or cup. Toss or process briefly with flour mixture.

4. Press mixture in a thin, even layer into the prepared pan.

5. Toss peaches with cinnamon and sugar, reserving 1 tbsp (15 ml) of sugar. Arrange fruit on the crust. Bake for 15 minutes.

6. Lower heat to 350°F (180°C). Combine egg with sour cream and remaining sugar, and spoon on top of the fruit. Continue baking about 10 minutes longer, until the crust is golden and the custard is set. Serve warm or cooled.

Makes 16–20 squares.

TIP:
• To peel peaches, dip in boiling water for about 30 seconds. Remove and plunge into ice water for a few seconds. Skins should slip off easily.

Cheesecake Squares
with Mixed Berry Sauce

Crust

2 cups	**graham cracker crumbs**	**500 ml**
6 tbsp	**butter,** *melted*	**90 ml**
¼ cup	**sugar**	**60 ml**

Filling

1½ lbs	**cream cheese**	**750 g**
1 cup	**sugar**	**250 ml**
3 tbsp	**flour**	**45 ml**
1 tbsp	**lemon rind,** *freshly grated*	**15 ml**
1 tsp	**vanilla**	**5 ml**
3	**eggs**	

Mixed Berry Sauce

2 cups each	**raspberries and blueberries,** *fresh or frozen*	**500 ml each**
1 tbsp	**lemon juice**	**15 ml**
¾ cup	**sugar** *(or to taste)*	**175 ml**
¼ cup	**orange liqueur** *or* **brandy** *(optional)*	**60 ml**

• *A treat to take to a party or potluck. Carry the berry sauce along in a separate container and spoon a bit on each square right before serving.*

1. Line a 10" x 15" (25 cm x 38 cm) jelly-roll pan or baking sheet with sides with parchment paper or foil. Preheat oven to 325°F (160°C).

2. Combine crust ingredients and spread in the pan, patting down to make an even layer. Bake in preheated oven for 10 minutes. Set aside to cool.

3. In a large bowl, using a hand mixer, combine cream cheese and sugar. Mix in flour, lemon rind, vanilla, and eggs.

4. Pour over prepared crust and bake in a 325°F (160°C) oven for 20–30 minutes or until filling in the centre of the pan is almost firm to the touch. Set aside to cool, then refrigerate before cutting into squares.

5. To make sauce, combine berries, juice and sugar in a blender or food processor and whirl until smooth. (If using frozen berries, thaw partially before using.) Add liqueur or brandy to taste, if you wish.

6. Press berry mixture through a sieve and store in covered containers in the refrigerator. Spoon over squares before serving.

Makes 16–20 squares.

TIP:
• The Mixed Berry Sauce will keep in the refrigerator for up to 4 weeks. Keep it on hand to use with pancakes, waffles, ice cream, frozen yogurt, and pound cake.

Bumbleberry Cobbler

6 cups	mixed berries	1.5 L
1/3 cup	sugar *(or to taste)*	75 ml
1 tsp	lemon zest, *grated*	5 ml
1 tbsp	lemon juice	15 ml
	buttermilk biscuit topping *(p. 133, modified; see Step 3, below)*	
1/4 cup	sugar	60 ml

TIP:

• For a glossy, crunchy finish, brush the biscuit topping with cream or beaten egg before baking and sprinkle with a tablespoon of brown sugar mixed with a pinch of cinnamon and grated lemon zest.

• *You won't find bumbleberries growing in the woods of Ontario's cottage country – but you will find bumbleberry pies. This is the name that has taken root to describe a concoction of mixed berries – blackberries, raspberries, blueberries, strawberries – and sometimes even including rhubarb and apples. Whatever's handy at baking time goes into the mix. Serve the cobbler warm with lightly sweetened, vanilla-flavoured whipped cream, custard, crème fraîche, sweetened yogurt, or vanilla ice cream.*

1. Thoroughly butter a 9" x 13" (23 cm x 33 cm) baking dish. Preheat oven to 375°F (190°C).

2. Toss the berries, 1/3 cup (75 ml) sugar, lemon zest, and juice together and place in the prepared baking dish.

3. Make the biscuit topping on p. 133, except omit the thyme and add 1/4 cup (60 ml) sugar to the dry ingredients.

4. Top the fruit with spoonfuls of the biscuit topping. Bake in preheated oven for 30–40 minutes, until the juices are bubbling and the topping is lightly browned. Serve warm.

Serves 8.

Summer Sensation
Ice Cream Pie

4 cups	**vanilla ice cream,** *slightly softened*	1 L
¾ cup	**frozen juice concentrate** *(see Tips, below)*	175 ml
1	**prepared crumb pie crust** *(graham cracker, Oreo, or vanilla crumbs)* *(9"/23 cm)*	
	fruit to garnish	

TIPS:
Try the following combinations, or invent one of your own:

• orange juice concentrate with mandarin orange sections on top

• raspberry concentrate with fresh raspberries or raspberry purée

• peach concentrate with peach slices

• lemonade concentrate, the pink kind with strawberries and the yellow kind with lemon slices

• limeade concentrate with lime slices or grated chocolate

• *Keep one of these refreshing pies on standby in the freezer. Match the filling with the season's fresh fruit.*

1. Mix ice cream and juice concentrate until blended. Spread evenly in prepared crust.

2. Cover tightly with plastic wrap. Freeze until firm, at least 4 hours.

3. Soften at room temperature about 10 minutes before serving. Top with fruit or a fruit sauce.

Makes about 6 servings.

VARIATION:
• For another amazing ice cream pie, bake a giant Decadent Fudge Cookie (p. 174) in a pie plate at 375°F (190°C) for 15 minutes. (Use about 2 cups/500 ml of dough.) Allow to cool, top with softened ice cream, and refreeze until serving time. Decorate the top with melted chocolate and toasted pecans if you wish.

Grilled Mint Julep Peaches

4	**small ripe peaches,** *(preferably freestone), peeled, halved, and pitted*	
	fresh mint, *chopped (for garnish)*	

Mint Julep Glaze

½ cup	**butter**	125 ml
½ cup	**bourbon**	125 ml
2 tbsp	**brown sugar**	30 ml
2 tbsp	**fresh mint,** *chopped*	30 ml

QUICK TRICK:
A Peachy Thick Shake (shown in photo, pp. 164–165), served in a chilled champagne glass, makes a cool, elegant summer dessert. To serve 4 people, combine about 1½ cups (375 ml) fresh peeled and sliced peaches with ¾ cup (175 ml) cold milk, ¼ cup (60 ml) orange, peach, or pineapple juice, and 1 tbsp (15 ml) honey in a blender. Process until smooth, then add 6 scoops vanilla ice cream and blend just until thick and smooth. Pour into glasses and garnish each with a peach slice.

● *The flavour of some fruits – such as peaches, mangoes, and pineapple – is intensified after a short time over the fire, especially when the fruit is brushed with a spicy, boozy glaze. Thread the peaches on bamboos skewers to grill them or, for a wonderful aroma, on long skinny cinnamon sticks. Fabulous served warm over ice cream.*

1. Soak cinnamon sticks or bamboo skewers in water for about an hour.

2. Combine glaze ingredients in a small saucepan, stirring over low heat for a couple of minutes until sugar and butter melt. Set aside for flavours to blend while you prepare the peaches.

3. Thread peach halves horizontally onto the cinnamon sticks or bamboo skewers, so that the cut sides will be exposed to the fire. (Depending on the size of the fruit, you may need to use 2 parallel skewers for each peach.)

4. Place skewered fruit on a clean, hot, lightly oiled grill over medium heat. Turn and baste with Mint Julep Glaze until peaches are warm and tender, about 10–12 minutes. Serve warm over ice cream with any remaining glaze poured over top and a sprinkling of chopped fresh mint.

Serves 4.

(Grilled Mint Julep Peaches are shown in the photo opposite p. 52.)

Totally Decadent Rice Pudding

½ cup	white rice *(preferably jasmine)*	125 ml
2 cups	whole milk	500 ml
1 cup	10% cream	250 ml
1	cinnamon stick *(3"/7 cm)*	
2	egg yolks	
½ cup	35% cream	125 ml
¼ cup	sugar	60 ml
pinch	salt	
pinch	nutmeg, *freshly grated*	

• *Rich, creamy, and thick. Serve with Strawberry Rhubarb Compote (p. 162) or Ginger Spiced Pears or Plums (p. 162) on top.*

1. Rinse rice and drain well. Combine in the top of a double boiler with the milk, 10% cream, and cinnamon stick. Set over simmering water and cook, uncovered, stirring occasionally, for 30–40 minutes, until rice is just tender and creamy.

2. In a small bowl whisk egg yolks with 35% cream and ladle in a few spoonfuls of hot, creamy rice. Stir the mixture back into the pot of rice, adding the sugar, salt, and nutmeg. Continue to cook gently in the double boiler for 5 minutes or so. Remove the cinnamon stick.

3. Set aside, covered, for 15 minutes. Serve warm or at room temperature.

Serves 4–6.

TIPS:

• For a less-fattening pudding, replace the whole milk and creams with 2 cups whole milk mixed with 1 cup of water.

• For a fragrant, East Indian-style pudding, use rinsed and soaked basmati rice. Lightly crush the grains first to release the starch. (This creates a creamier consistency.) Flavour the milk with green cardamom pods and cinnamon.

• When refrigerated overnight, the pudding becomes very thick; thin out with additional milk or cream.

• Instead of topping the pudding with fruit, add ¼ cup (60 ml) raisins, dried cranberries, or dried cherries during the last 5 minutes of cooking.

Maple Caramel Corn

1½ cups	sugar	375 ml
½ cup	water	125 ml
½ cup	maple syrup	125 ml
3 tbsp	butter	45 ml
2 tbsp	vinegar	30 ml
½ tsp	salt	2 ml
½ tsp	baking soda	2 ml
8 cups	popped corn, *no salt, no butter*	2 L
1 cup	pecans, *roughly chopped*	250 ml

TIP:

• For over-the-top delicious, melt semi-sweet chocolate and pour over the cooled caramel corn. Set on cookie sheet for chocolate to harden.

• *Fun to make, these caramel popcorn-and-nut clusters are even better than the storebought kind.*

1. Combine sugar, water, maple syrup, butter, vinegar, and salt in a small heavy saucepan. Cook over high heat for about 10 minutes until a spoonful of the mixture forms a hard ball when dropped into ice water or the mixture registers 260°F (125°C) on a candy thermometer.

2. Remove pan from heat and stir in baking soda. The mixture will foam up and become creamy.

3. Place the popped corn and pecans in a large bowl. Pour the caramel syrup over top and stir to coat evenly. Spread on a large cookie sheet to cool.

Makes about 8 cups (2 L).

QUICK TRICK:

S'mores are a summer classic – as much after-dinner entertainment as dessert. You'll need lots of large marshmallows, graham crackers – or, if you want to get fancy, thin gingersnaps – and squares of dark chocolate. Toast a marshmallow over the fire until it's golden outside and molten inside, then plop it onto a graham cracker. Top with a piece of chocolate and another graham cracker. Eat instantly.

VARIATION: Skip the square of chocolate and squish the toasted marshmallow between two Decadent Fudge Cookies (p. 174).

Index

Recipe variations and Quick Tricks have been indexed; therefore, when looking for a recipe on a page, also check the sections in coloured type.

*Recipe variations and Quick Tricks have been indexed; therefore, when looking for a recipe on a page, also check the sections in coloured type.

Recipe variations and Quick Tricks have been indexed; therefore, when looking for a recipe on a page, also check the sections in coloured type.

*Recipe variations and Quick Tricks have been indexed; therefore, when looking for a recipe on a page, also check the sections in coloured type.

*Recipe variations and Quick Tricks have been indexed; therefore, when looking for a recipe on a page, also check the sections in coloured type.

*Recipe variations and Quick Tricks have been indexed; therefore, when looking for a recipe on a page, also check the sections in coloured type.

*Recipe variations and Quick Tricks have been indexed; therefore, when looking for a recipe on a page, also check the sections in coloured type.